SOMERSE. ..... ILLDS
IN THE
SECOND WORLD WAR

Other areas covered in the Airfield series include:

Cambridgeshire
Cumbria, including the Isle of Man
Devon & Cornwall
Dorset
Essex
Gloucestershire
Hampshire
Herefordshire and Worcestershire
Hertfordshire & Bedfordshire
Kent
Lancashire
Leicestershire & Rutland
Lincolnshire
Norfolk
Northamptonshire
North-East England
Nottinghamshire & Derbyshire
Oxfordshire
Suffolk
Surrey
Sussex
Thames Valley
Warwickshire
Wiltshire
Yorkshire

SOMERSET AIRFIELDS IN THE SECOND WORLD WAR

David Berryman

COUNTRYSIDE BOOKS
NEWBURY, BERKSHIRE

First published 2006
© David Berryman 2006

COUNTRYSIDE BOOKS
3 Catherine Road
Newbury, Berkshire

To view our complete range of books,
please visit us at
www. countrysidebooks co.uk

For my daughter, Genevieve,
for her support and inspiration

ISBN 1 85306 864 0
EAN 978 1 85306 864 5

The cover picture shows Westland Whirlwind fighters
taking off from Charmy Down during the autumn of 1941
and is from an original painting by Colin Doggett

Designed by Mon Mohan
Produced through MRM Associates Ltd, Reading
Typeset by Jean Cussons Typesetting, Diss, Norfolk
Printed by Woolnough Bookbinding Ltd., Irthlingborough

CONTENTS

MAP OF SOMERSET'S SECOND WORLD WAR AIRFIELDS

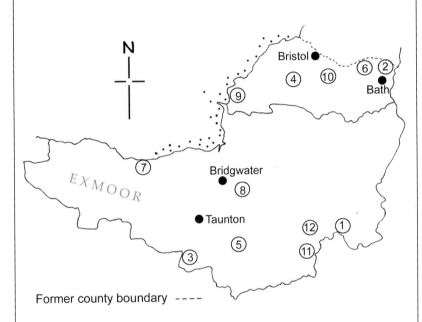

Former county boundary - - - -

KEY TO MAP

1	Charlton Horethorne	7	Watchet
2	Charmy Down	8	Weston Zoyland
3	Culmhead (Church Stanton)	9	Weston-super-Mare
4	Lulsgate Botton (Broadfield Down)	10	Whitchurch
5	Merryfield (Isle Abbots)	11	Yeovil
6	North Stoke	12	Yeovilton

ACKNOWLEDGEMENTS

I would like to thank the following individuals and organizations that have assisted me in writing this book:

Bath Blitz Memorial Project
Captain Eric Brown, RN (retd)
Colin Cruddas
Terry Heffernan
Neil Holt
Nick Stroud and the team at *Aeroplane Magazine*
MoD Library, Whitehall
Jeanette Powell, MoD
Jean Buckberry, Senior Librarian, RAF College Cranwell
British Aerospace
Somerset Museum and Library Service
Museum of Army Flying, Middle Wallop
National Archives, Kew
RAF Museum, Hendon
Wiltshire County Libraries

Nigel Clarke of Nigel J. Clarke Publications (for more information about their books and photographs, see www.njcpublications.co.uk)

Michael Turner (for more details and information about Michael's work, visit www.studio88.co.uk)

I would also like to thank Nicholas Battle and his team at Countryside Books for their help and encouragement, and my wife, Karen, for her typing skills and her support in helping me compile this manuscript.

I
SETTING THE SCENE

Somerset has long been associated with agriculture, along with industry, and it was these two areas of activity that brought about some of the earliest awakenings of aviation in Britain. One of the pioneers of aviation technology, John Stringfellow, lived in the county during the 19th century.

Stringfellow was born in Sheffield and moved to Chard in Somerset with his father in 1829. Making machinery and bobbins for the local lace-making industry there, he started to research and develop lightweight steam engines. He met William Henson, who had similarly moved from Nottingham, and whose imagination had also moved from lace-making machinery to other products and ideas. These included a flying machine that could carry trade over long distances. With the support of Stringfellow, Henson patented an aerial steam carriage in 1842 and set up the Aerial Transit Company to raise funds to finance the project. However, this vision – some 60 years before the Wright Brothers' first flight – was ahead of its time, and lack of success resulted in Henson leaving for the USA. Nevertheless Stringfellow persevered, and in 1848 he designed and built the first aeroplane to be flown under its own power, albeit unmanned. It weighed 9 lbs, had a wing span of 10 feet, and was powered by a lightweight steam engine. His power unit later won the first gold medal to be awarded by the Aeronautical Society when it was formed in 1866. The work of these two Somerset aeronautical pioneers undoubtedly inspired others in proving that heavier than air flight was possible.

The first manned powered flight in Britain took place some 60 years after the first successful flight of Stringfellow's model, when, on 16 October 1908, Samuel F. Cody flew an aeroplane that he had himself designed, from Laffan's Plain, Farnborough. Other aeroplane designs followed, and the number of manufacturers proliferated. One of the first of these was the Bristol and Colonial Aeroplane Company, which was established in February 1910, just across the Somerset-Gloucestershire border at Filton.

The company also set up a flying school at Larkhill in Wiltshire, and it was from there that a number of pioneering long-distance flights were made. Graham Gilmour, a company pilot, set off with co-pilot Gordon England on one such flight on 12 April 1911, in a Bristol Boxkite, heading for Somerset. After getting disorientated and following the wrong railway lines, they eventually landed at Henstridge, where they spent the night. From there they finally got to Yeovil, where they were welcomed by crowds at the sports field. These pioneering flights continued, and aeroplanes were gradually to be seen by more and more people; some even had the chance to fly in them! The outbreak of the Great War just a few years later, however, would transform not just aviation, but the country as a whole, including the county of Somerset.

The Westland Aircraft Works was set up at Yeovil in 1915, and soon began manufacturing hundreds of aircraft for the Royal

Bristol Boxkites pioneered flying in Somerset. (Author)

Flying Corps and Royal Naval Air Service, production continuing throughout the war. Despite the rapid post-war reduction in the armed forces and in the demand for military aeroplanes, Westland somehow managed to keep going throughout the 1920s and 1930s.

Nonetheless, the surplus military aircraft that became available enabled a number of small airlines and airfreight businesses to get started. Alan Cobham started travelling the country at this time, giving joy-rides and mounting flying displays. His first tour of the West Country was made in 1922, with a visit to the May Fair at Wells, during which a record was set for the highest number of passengers taken up by a single aircraft in one day: 153, which is 77 flights. During the next stop, at Bridgwater, members of the team undertook wing-walking, probably for the first time in Britain. Cobham went on to mount a flying circus, which included aerobatics and crazy flying displays as well as joy rides offered to the public. These events received widespread publicity and popularized aviation.

Cobham encouraged local authorities to dedicate specific areas to flying, and some of these later became civic airports. In 1930 Bristol established its first airport at Whitchurch, to the south of the

Avro 504s were flown by the pilots of Cobham's Flying Circus. (Aeroplane)

city, in Somerset, and Weston-super-Mare Airport was started in the mid-1930s.

Meanwhile, British military aviation had revived during the 1930s with the establishment of the RAF Expansion Scheme. This was initiated by the government, prompted by the threat posed by the rapid increase in strength of the German air force, the Luftwaffe.

When Hitler came to power in 1933, Germany had been disarmed for thirteen years, and although its army consisted of 100,000 men, it had no tanks, no aeroplanes and very little in the way of artillery. By 1939 it was militarily one of the most powerful nations in Europe, and was able to mobilise and equip armed forces of some 4 million men.

During the intervening period, Hitler's government had embarked on a massive rearmament programme. Initially, the build-up complied with the terms of the Versailles Treaty, which limited the size of Germany's armed forces and its equipment. Warships were built within a prescribed tonnage limit (which resulted in the 'pocket battleships' such as the *Graf Spee*) and military aircraft were of restricted performance.

There was, therefore, a sudden interest in racers, mail-planes and airliners in Germany that eventually became, when all pretext was

Heinkel He111s were involved in many raids on Somerset. (Aeroplane)

dropped a few years later, fighters, bombers and military transports.

These types included the Bf109 fighter, which 'officially' was designed as a racer. The aircraft did, in fact, win a number of competitions and in November 1937 established a new world airspeed record of 379.4 mph that was to stand for two years. The aircraft went on to become the mainstay of the Luftwaffe fighter squadrons for the majority of the wartime period, some 35,000 being built in two main versions. The type's originator, Willi Messerschmitt, was the Chief Designer of the Bayerische Flugzengwerke, and by the time that his next design, the Bf110, was produced in 1936, there was no pretence that it was anything other than a twin-engined day fighter. The type enjoyed limited success in this role, but it was subsequently employed as a light bomber and night fighter. In July 1938 Willi Messerschmitt was appointed Chairman and Managing Director of the Bayerische Flugzengwerke, and the company's name was changed to Messerschmitt AG. New designs produced by the company from that date were given 'Me' rather than 'Bf' designations.

The Luftwaffe's main transport aircraft, the Junkers Ju52 tri-motor, was, in fact, one of the few genuinely civil aircraft produced in Germany during the 1930s. Designed as an airliner, it first flew in April 1931 and entered service with Lufthansa the following year. Fitted with armament, the type served as a bomber with the Luftwaffe's Condor Legion during the Spanish Civil War, but subsequently formed the backbone of the Luftwaffe's transport fleet during the Second World War.

The Heinkel He111 twin-engined bomber was ostensibly produced as a civil airliner for Lufthansa, and a few even entered service as internal passenger-carrying routes in 1934. However, it was not long before the bomber version appeared, and the aircraft became the major Luftwaffe bomber of the early war period, seeing action over the Low Countries and France, and during the Battle of Britain. Later used as a night-bomber and, ironically, as a transport, the type remained in production until autumn 1944.

The other main German bomber types that were in service with the Luftwaffe in 1939, such as the Junkers Ju33 and Dornier Do17 twin-engined bombers and the Ju87 'Stuka' dive-bomber, were

The Luftwaffe's feared Messerschmitt Bf109. This captured example was on display at a local Rover garage. (Aeroplane)

designed from the outset as military aircraft, as by 1936 any German compliance with the Versailles Treaty had been dropped.

Still suffering from the effects of post-war cutbacks, the RAF of the early 1930s had a strength of only 850 aircraft, a number based on balancing the only European air force that could pose a threat to Britain – that of France. The rapid rearmament of Germany had come as an unpleasant shock, particularly in terms of the capabilities of its equipment, not just its numbers. In 1934 the fastest RAF fighter was the Hawker Fury biplane at 207 mph, and the most potent was the Handley Page Heyford biplane bomber, which had a bomb load of 3,000 lbs and a range of 500 miles. In contrast the Luftwaffe's Me109 monoplane fighter, which flew the following year, had a maximum speed of 290 mph, and, although its monoplane Heinkel He111 had a bomb load equivalent to the Heyford, it was much faster, with a range of 800 miles.

The pre-war expansion of the RAF was initiated by Air Chief Marshal Sir Robert Brooke Popham, Commander in Chief of the Air Defence of Great Britain. The Expansion scheme was put into effect in thirteen stages, each one alphabetically coded. Scheme A extended fighter cover northwards to include the industrial regions. Others subsequently added more bomber squadrons (and

The Handley Page Heyford, state of the art British bomber of 1934. (Aeroplane)

airfields for them to operate from), formed four RAF Commands in 1936 (Fighter, Bomber, Coastal, and Training), and in 1938 called for 2,373 front-line aircraft in 152 squadrons and reorganized flying training.

The British aircraft industry was able to respond to orders from the government for aircraft not only of established designs but also new types to meet more advanced specifications. As a result the Hurricane and the Spitfire were produced, along with light bombers such as the Blenheim and later the Mosquito, as well as heavier types. In Somerset the Westland Aircraft Company was busy making the Lysander, an advanced single-engined high-wing monoplane that was evolved for the army co-operation role. Its excellent handling and manœuvrability at low speeds and its ability to operate from small airfields made it ideal for its role, and it was later adapted for other tasks, such as air-sea rescue and covert operations. The company also licence-built other types, and later undertook conversions and specialist work such as the battle-damage repair of fighter aircraft.

The result of this increase in British aircraft production during the late 1930s meant that when war did come the RAF had some 2,000 aircraft in front-line service and in the region of another 2,200 in reserve. Some were biplanes, but the majority were modern

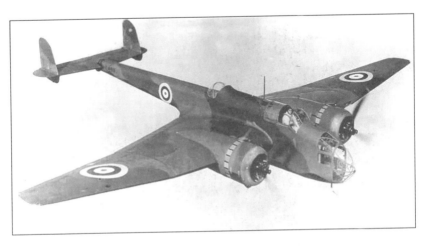

The Handley Page Hampden followed the Heyford into service with the RAF in 1936. (Aeroplane)

Spitfires were in production in the late 1930s to counter the Bf 109. (Aeroplane)

monoplanes such as the 300 mph Hurricane and Spitfire fighters, and the Vickers Wellingtons and Handley Page Hampden bombers, that could take a 4,0000 lb bomb load well into Germany at over 200 mph. The Luftwaffe confronting it had 4,000 front-line aircraft with a further 1,000 reserves, but, although numerically superior, it could not match the training, spirit and courage of the Royal Air Force.

The RAF presence in Somerset before the war was limited to anti-aircraft training and support. One of the major anti-aircraft training centres was at Doniford Camp, Watchet. Firing camps were held there each summer from 1928, which meant that liaison and support aircraft needed an airfield nearby. This was later supplemented and subsequently replaced by Weston Zoyland, which developed as an RAF airfield from 1939. As the station's role changed the target support aircraft were supplemented by training and transport types.

In 1939 Weston Zoyland and the works airfield at Yeovil, along with the civil airports at Weston-super-Mare and Whitchurch, were the only operational airfields in Somerset. Flying at the two latter

18

was swiftly curtailed as a consequence of the restrictions on civil flying that came in immediately on the outbreak of war. Although Weston was then used for training, Whitchurch was to continue as a civil airport, becoming the main civil terminus for the UK, and the headquarters of BOAC for the duration of the war. New airfields started to appear in the county, initially for training, such as Lulsgate Bottom and Yeovilton in 1940, but as hostile bombers began to appear in the region, fighter airfields were built, such as Charmy Down, Culmhead and Charlton Horethorne. Although Merryfield was built as a bomber base, it later became a transport base, and was used during the D-Day invasion along with Weston Zoyland. Other Somerset airfields, such as Charmy Down, played a role in Operation Overlord by acting as bases for tactical support, and their units took the war into the Third Reich itself.

At the end of the Great War there were some 300 airfields in Britain. The vast majority of these (250 or so) were given up during 1919 and 1920, and by 1924 there were only 27 military and 17 civil airfields in the country. With the advent of the RAF Expansion Scheme, an organization was needed to satisfy the demand for new airfields. This was found in the Works Directorate of the Air Ministry, that was formed in 1934 to maintain existing airfields and to build new ones.

However, funds were still short: in 1935, out of an Air Ministry budget of £27.5 million, only some £5 million was spent on works, which included ground training establishments and headquarters buildings as well as airfields. The situation gradually improved, and the proportion spent on airfields of the overall budget was to increase over the following years, reaching a peak of £145 million in 1942.

The airfield construction programme was a huge undertaking and one of the major wartime projects in the UK. Under the co-ordination of the Works Directorate, the actual work was largely undertaken by construction companies such as Laing, McAlpine, Taylor Woodrow, and Wimpey, which owed much of their subsequent success to this essential wartime work. Although there was a shortage of civil engineering plant and equipment initially, this increasingly became available from the USA. Much of the labour to operate the equipment was provided by the Ministry of Labour and National Service, whose minister, Ernest Bevan,

19

decreed in 1942 that 28,000 building workers who were due to be called up into the armed forces be temporarily retained by the industry on airfield construction. At its peak some 60,000 men were employed on the programme. In December 1942, 510 airfields were in operation in Britain, with 106 under construction, and a further 54 airfield sites being prepared.

The building of a typical airfield employed over one thousand men and took eight months to complete. After every tree was removed from the site, hedgerows were grubbed out and any remaining obstructions were bulldozed or demolished. Hollows and ditches were filled and the surface roughly levelled. Ploughs were often then used to prepare the ground for the next stage, which was the final planing of the earth by graders, so that no gradient was of more than a one-in-sixty in slope.

The first surfaces to be laid were generally those of the perimeter track, to enable access to the site of the runway and other parts of the airfield by road vehicles carrying hardcore and other materials. Hardened runways were felt to be a luxury by the RAF planners during the 1930s, a firm grass surface being felt sufficient for normal aircraft operations. However, with aircraft all-up weights gradually increasing, it was eventually admitted that concrete runways ought to be provided for the heavier types. Nonetheless, relatively few RAF airfields had hard runways by the time war broke out in 1939. It was soon specified that Class A bomber airfields should be provided with three good concrete and tarmac runways, and by late 1940 hardened runways became an important feature of all new airfields.

While one sub-contractor was laying hardcore for the concrete runways that were subsequently to be coated in layers of tarmac, others would be undertaking work such as laying hard-standings and erecting hangars. At least one hangar would usually be put up fairly early on, simply for the practical purpose of providing undercover storage for construction plant and equipment. The technical and domestic sites would also be started at this time, barrack accommodation being an early priority for housing the construction workers while work proceeded!

Large numbers of other buildings and installations followed, such as the control tower, flight operations, briefing rooms, stores, workshops, MT sheds, messes, magazines, bomb dumps, bulk fuel storage, and airfield defences. Added to these were airfield, runway and approach lighting systems, along with radio and radio installations. Other often overlooked but essential services were also provided, such as water, electricity, mains sewerage, and waste drainage.

By 1945 in the region of 360,000 acres of British soil were occupied by airfields. To produce their runways, perimeter tracks and dispersals, some 160 million square yards of concrete were laid. According to Sir Archibald Sinclair, Secretary of State for Air, this equated to a 30 foot wide highway stretching 9,000 miles from London to Peking. Additionally, 30 million tons of hardcore, 18 million cubic feet of wood, and 336,000 miles of electricity cables were consumed by this mammoth undertaking.

In addition to the main airfields, supplementary ones evolved, particularly for the Maintenance Units (MUs) and the flying training schools. The MUs stored many aircraft in their hangars, either as reserves, or because the airframes were undergoing repairs or modification. The main sites became busy soon after the war started, and as they began to fill up they presented a tempting target to enemy bombers. Satellite landing grounds (SLGs) were therefore sought, to which some of the stored aircraft could be dispersed. As in the case of North Stoke, these were usually just fields or grassed areas provided with minimum preparation before aircraft began to arrive. Adjacent wooded areas were an added advantage for camouflaging the stored aircraft.

Relief landing grounds (RLGs) were set up by flying training units to ease the congestion that was often present with as many as 100 trainers operating from a typical flying training station. The RLGs were usually used for take-off and landing practice and for circuit flying. They also provided useful locations for night flying practice, well away from the main airfield with its attendant risks of night attacks by enemy bombers attracted by the lights of the flare path.

Other airfields included dummy ones, which were built to act as decoys, drawing attention away from the real airfields. They were of two main categories: K sites for daylight use, and Q sites for night-time. The former were more complex, as they had to simulate the real thing during the day and to have convincing-looking runways, buildings and installations, including road vehicles and aircraft. The Q sites were easier to construct, as they had to reproduce the lighting of an airfield at night, which during blackout conditions was minimal anyway. By the end of 1941, 322 of the Luftwaffe's attacks had been made on decoys, compared with 304 on genuine airfields. Both types of decoy were therefore extremely successful. As more actual airfields were built, so too were more decoys. Airfield decoy sites in Somerset included Bleadon (to divert attacks from Weston-super-Mare) and Kings Moor, (near Yeovilton).

As the war progressed, more sophisticated decoys were developed to keep enemy aircrews interested. Two such examples, Starfish and QL sites, were night decoys. Starfish or special fire (SF) sites were designed so that trays of fuel could be lit and controlled by RAF personnel in a bunker, as it was noticed that German bomber crews were attracted by fires at night. Trays and baskets containing a variety of materials such as petrol, wood and straw

Messerschmitt Bf110s often acted as pathfinders for the Luftwaffe's bombers. (Aeroplane)

produced different effects to simulate burning airfield buildings or installations. QL sites had special lighting effects that could be used alone or with SF sites to add realism. These ranged from light boxes to replicate the lights of a building as seen through windows left open in the blackout, to 'hares and rabbits', which consisted of lights on a rig that travelled along the ground or on a gantry to simulate an aircraft taxying or taking off. Others replicated the lights of road vehicles. Further realism was often added to the sites in the form of dummy flare paths and runway approach lighting. The advantage of these sites was that they could be built anywhere – well away from towns or other habitation, for example – and in any terrain.

As well as simulating airfields, Starfish and QL sites were also established to protect army bases and industrial areas. A ring of ten sites was built around Bristol, to divert bombers away from the city and its docks, including a huge and complex QL/SF site in the Mendip Hills that simulated Temple Meads railway station and marshalling yards.

Although the Americans were reluctant to get involved in the Second World War, US troops arrived in Britain only seven weeks after the Japanese had provoked their involvement by bombing Pearl Harbor in December 1941. From February 1942, a steady flow of US military personnel and equipment started to cross the Atlantic, mainly in convoys of troop ships and cargo vessels. Arriving in the bomb-damaged port of Liverpool must have brought home to the American troops just what Britain had endured during two years of war. To ease congestion in other parts of the country, the American ground units were moved mainly to the southern and western parts of Britain, and soon US Army hutted camps were sprouting up in Somerset, as well as Cornwall, Devon, Wiltshire and Gloucestershire. From the initial trickle, a flow developed in 1943 and by January 1944 there were over 750,000 US Army personnel in the UK. Through the following spring and early summer the numbers increased as the Allies prepared for the invasion of France, and in May 1944 well over 1.5 million US service personnel were based in Britain.

Advance units of the United States Army Air Force (USAAF) began to arrive in the UK in May 1942. Based mainly in East Anglia under the control of the US Eighth Air Force, which was the strategic bombing formation of the USAAF in Britain, US aircraft were seldom seen in the West Country. This changed in October 1943, when the US Ninth Air Force was formed, with its headquarters at Sunninghill Park, Ascot. This was to become the US tactical air formation in preparation for the Allied invasion of northern Europe, and its squadrons of reconnaissance, fighter bomber and troop-carrying aircraft were to provide direct support to US and Allied troops.

Three airfields in Somerset were handed over to the Ninth Air Force in late 1943 and early 1944, to become US bases. Charmy Down was established as Station 487 and used as the Fourth Tactical Air Depot, for the repair, maintenance, and storage of aircraft. In early 1944 it became the home of the 422nd Night Fighter Squadron. Merryfield and later Weston Zoyland were allocated to the IXth Troop Carrier Command for the operation of Douglas C-47 Skytrains and Waco Hadrian gliders, which subsequently took part in the D-Day landings before moving to Europe. Other US aircraft that were regularly to be seen in Somerset during this time were the Piper L-4 Cubs and Stinson L-5 Sentinel light liaison aircraft which flew between the main airfields and US Army formation HQs. Most divisions, brigades, and corps HQs had facilities to operate them, usually amounting to just a suitable field nearby. Examples of these include Hestercombe House, near Taunton (the HQ of V Corps), Redlynch House, near Bruton (the HQ of Third Armoured Division), and Watchet, near the Doniford anti-aircraft gunnery ranges.

Somerset was not in the front-line during the early stages of the Second World War, and its airfields initially fulfilled a training and support role. However, it was not long before fighters were stationed in the county as part of the defences against enemy air attacks. In the meantime the county's aircraft factories, such as the Westland works at Yeovil and Bristols at Old Mixon, carried on working, turning out the aeroplanes that were essential for the RAF and Fleet Air Arm (FAA). Training continued, as at Lulsgate, to maintain the supply of pilots to the RAF, and at Yeovilton, to produce combat-ready FAA squadrons that would later undertake operations around the world. The units based on Somerset's airfields were eventually to go on the offensive and take the war to the enemy as the balance of air power shifted in favour of the

Allies. Operations from the county's airfields gradually increased in momentum and its units made a significant contribution to the outstanding success of the Normandy landings, when the Allies were once again to set foot on the Continent, and push the Germans back into their homeland.

2

CHARLTON HORETHORNE

2 miles north-west of the village so named
ST 643244

Although later a Naval Air Station, Charlton Horethorne was originally planned by the RAF. It was envisaged as a satellite for RAF Exeter, a main operational station under 10 Group, Fighter Command. Construction of the buildings and preparation of the airfield's surface started during the summer of 1941, and most of the work was completed by the following spring. Charlton Horethorne was more of a landing ground than a fully developed airfield, as it had a grass surface and, apart from a control (or watch) tower and two blister hangars, few buildings on the main site. Blast pens were built to provide protection to dispersed fighters from air attack.

An advance party arrived from RAF Exeter on 1 June 1942, and the most important event for any service establishment occurred on 30 June, when the NAAFI opened. On 10 July 1942, Charlton Horethorne opened as a RAF station under 10 Group, commanded by Squadron Leader F.B. Lowe. By this time, the airfield had been made available for the use of the Royal Navy, and later that day two naval units arrived – Nos. 886 and 887 Squadrons, both with Fulmars. However, 887 did not stay long, departing for St. Merryn on 25 July.

On 27 July an advance party of 790 Squadron arrived at Charlton Horethorne to re-form the unit there, it having previously been

26

Oxfords were flown by 790 Squadron from Charlton Horethorne. (Aeroplane)

disbanded at Macrihanish. It was re-formed as part of the Fighter Direction School, based eight miles away at Yeovilton. The squadron's role was that of fighter interception training for trainee Air Direction Radar (ADR) operators, or fighter controllers, and also for the pilots of Fleet Air Arm fighter squadrons. For this purpose it was equipped with Oxfords and Fulmars. With the arrival on the following day of the squadron's main party and its aircraft, 790 began what was to be a productive and lengthy stay at Charlton Horethorne, remaining at the base for the rest of the war, apart from one short detachment.

Ground defence of the station was put into the hands of the Somerset Light Infantry, who prepared trenches, hardpoints and machine gun positions. The Fulmars of 886 Squadron moved out on 10 August 1942, having been transferred to Turnhouse. On the following day 891 Squadron arrived, a single-seat fighter unit equipped with six Sea Hurricane 1bs. The unit had formed at Lee-on-Solent the previous month and was earmarked for front-line service. It spent its time at Charlton Horethorne preparing for carrier operations. As with many other fighter squadrons that came through the station, the unit spent much of its time on air interception training with 790 Squadron and the rest of the Fighter Direction School. Unfortunately one of 891's aircraft became the first to crash at Charlton Horethorne, making a crash landing on the airfield on 17 August. The pilot was uninjured and the Sea Hurricane was repairable.

There was some excitement on the airfield in early September when on the 3rd an enemy aircraft was spotted by the lookouts at No. 1 Gun Position. However, it was out of range. It later transpired that the aircraft had dropped bombs at Castle Cary.

A week later, on 9 September 1942, 891 Squadron was on the move again, as it transferred to St Merryn in Cornwall. (The unit later embarked aboard HMS *Dasher* to take part in Operation Torch, the North African landings, providing air cover over the invasion

Martlets were flown by 893 Squadron from the airfield. (Aeroplane)

beaches.) They exchanged at Charlton Horethorne with 893 Squadron, who flew in their US-built Grumman Martlets later that day. The unit was busy working up, having been formed at Donibristle on 15 June, and was awaiting an operational deployment. This came on 3 October, when two Harrow transports of 782 Squadron arrived to take the unit's stores and equipment to Hatston in the Orkneys. However, the 782 Squadron pilots decided that the main runway was not long enough to allow a fully-loaded Harrow to take off, so the transports were flown to Yeovilton and loaded there. The move was eventually made on 6 October, and on 21 October the squadron embarked aboard HMS *Formidable*, which also later took part in Operation Torch during which the Martlets spotted and attacked a U-boat.

A distressing accident occurred on the airfield on 1 October, when a taxying Fulmar collided with a motorcycle combination being ridden by a postman delivering mail to the station. Although he survived, one of the unfortunate postman's arms was severed by the Fulmar's propeller. The next arrival at the airfield was 879 Squadron, on 10 October. Having been formed at St Merryn nine days earlier with Fulmars, the unit spent five weeks working up at Charlton Horethorne before moving on. They went to Old Sarum on 18 November, where they were to undertake ground support training at the School of Army Co-operation. The squadron later sailed to the Mediterranean aboard HMS *Attacker* and flew operations in support of the Salerno landings in Sicily in September 1943. They were followed by another Fulmar unit, 809 Squadron, which arrived at Charlton Horethorne on 26 November on transfer from Macrihanish. Leaving again on 9 December for Doncaster, 809 Squadron also subsequently took part in the North African landings.

On 1 December 1942 Charlton Horethorne was formally transferred from 10 Group to the Admiralty, as the RAF had no further need for it. It was then formally commissioned as HMS *Heron II*, a satellite of RNAS Yeovilton. As the resident unit, 790 Squadron continued with its training as part of the Fighter Direction School. Ground courses were held at the main school at Yeovilton and then moved on to the flying phase with 790 Squadron, which was held at *Heron II* to avoid congestion at the main station. With 790 Squadron the students gained practical

A Fulmar, as flown by 790 and 879 Squadrons. (Aeroplane)

experience of fighter direction, using Oxfords to represent bombers and Fulmars for the intercepting fighters. They also flew in the aircraft, to gain experience from the pilot's viewpoint.

Other units continued to pass through, such as 897 Squadron on 11 January 1943. Formed on Sea Hurricanes the month before, the unit practised and trained with 790 Squadron, before moving to St Merryn on 22 March, where it received Seafires. (It later took part in the Salerno operation.)

More construction work took place at *Heron II* in 1943. A new watch tower was built, providing a better view of the airfield, the surface of which was improved and regraded, and five runways were laid out, mown into the grass surface. Two over-blister and two smaller hangars were added, along with a stores and living quarters.

On 6 April 1943, 804 Squadron moved in from Hatston, having disembarked its Sea Hurricanes from HMS *Dasher*. The unit had provided fighter escorts during the North African landings in November 1942. It trained at its new base until 20 June, when it moved on to Eglington in Scotland, to receive Grumman Hellcats.

The squadron later took part in the Atlantic convoys. It was replaced at *Heron II* by 887 Squadron, on transfer from Yeovilton, on 10 July. Its Fulmars stayed for a few weeks' training with 790 Squadron, before transferring to St Merryn on 25 July. There it received Seafires, and subsequently flew from escort carriers in the Mediterranean.

What was to be a longer-term resident, 780 Squadron, transferred in on 9 October 1943. Although it was originally formed at Eastleigh as a Conversion Course Squadron to convert civilian-trained pilots to naval standards, the unit's main task had evolved into that of converting operational biplane pilots from the Swordfish and Albacores to the Brewster Barracuda monoplane torpedo bomber, which saw only limited service. Following its move to Somerset, the unit assumed a more traditional training role, and for this was equipped with the de Havilland Tiger Moth, Miles Master II and North American Harvard trainers. It also had a few Fairey Swordfish and Bristol Blenheims. The unit was joined a few weeks later by 794 Squadron, which arrived on 1 December on transfer from Henstridge. With 16 Sea Hurricanes, four Masters, four Defiants and four Martinets, the squadron acted as a target-towing and air-firing training unit for the Fighter School at

Tiger Moths were used by 780 Squadron for initial training. (Aeroplane)

Amongst several different types flown by 794 Squadron from Charlton Horethorne was the Defiant Target Tug. (Aeroplane)

Yeovilton. It remained at its new base until it was disbanded on 30 June the following year.

Training continued at Charlton Horethorne into 1944. On 10 February, 765 Squadron came into being. Having been disbanded at Sandbanks in Dorset as a seaplane training school, it was re-formed at *Heron II* as the Travelling Recording Unit. Its main purpose was to record the efficiency of naval radar units and to assist in the calibration of their equipment. The unit also had a secondary role, which was that of long-range maritime reconnaissance, and was one of the very few Fleet Air Arm squadrons to fly the Vickers Wellington twin-engined bomber. However, because of the airfield's limitations, the Wellingtons couldn't fly from Charlton Horethorne unless weather conditions were perfect and the aircraft was lightly-loaded. The unit moved on to Lee-on-Solent on 18 March, and later moved to the Mediterranean.

By the summer of 1944, 790 Squadron was still flying the Oxford, but in June its Fulmars were replaced by the more advanced Fairey

Firefly. On 10 August the unit was detached to Culmhead, returning on 26 September.

Towards the end of November 780 Squadron moved to Lee-on-Solent, leaving 790 as sole resident, to carry on fulfilling its training duties into 1945. In February, the unit started to receive the first examples of the Spitfire Vb, and these were followed in early March by early Seafires (Marks Ib and IIc). However, that spring, it was agreed that the RAF would make Zeals in Wiltshire available to the Fleet Air Arm, in exchange for Charlton Horethorne. Accordingly, on 1 April 1945, 790 Squadron started leaving for its new base at Zeals. Charlton Horethorne was then taken over by 42 Group, RAF Maintenance Command, who used it for the storage of ammunition as one of the sub-depots of No. 11 Maintenance Unit at Chilmark. This continued until the end of 1947, when the site was cleared of munitions. It was transferred to the control of RAF Old Sarum in June 1948 as a satellite training airfield. The station was held on a Care and Maintenance basis for a while, but was then de-requisitioned and returned to farmland. Today there are few signs of the former airfield. A number of its buildings were taken over by Charlton Hill Farm and can still be seen, along with the remains of some of the fighter pens.

3
CHARMY DOWN

3 miles north of Bath
ST 764700

The area of Charmy Down forms a plateau in the hills north of
Bath. Whereas other plateaux in the area tend to be long and thin,
Charmy Down has length and breadth, being almost a mile from
west to east, and two thirds of a mile from north to south. It is
bordered on almost all sides by steep gradients, but it was decided
in 1939 that with careful planning an airfield could be built there.
The site had been chosen as a satellite for the Maintenance Unit at
Colerne, a few miles away to the east, but, by the time work started
on the construction of Charmy Down airfield in 1940, Colerne had
been selected as a sector station by 10 Group Fighter Command.
Charmy Down was therefore built as a fighter base, with 39 aircraft
dispersals – 12 double fighter pens and 15 single dispersals –
running off a tarmac perimeter track. Twelve blister hangars were
erected around the airfield and a Bellman hangar was built on the
main technical site, located on its eastern side. The runways were
originally marked out on the graded grass surface, but three tarmac
runways were laid in 1941. The main one, of 4,350 feet, ran from
south-east to north-west; the secondary, of 4,050 feet, from south-
west to north-east, and the third, of 2,799 feet, from north to south.

The main site (no. 1) was situated on the western side of the
airfield, and included the watch office (or control tower), briefing
rooms and other operational buildings. There were several living

sites, the main one being to the north-west of the airfield, beside Hartley Farm, with others to the west of that, on both sides of the A46 road that runs up a valley from the south and heads off to the west of the airfield.

The first aircraft to use the newly-opened airfield were the Hurricanes of 87 Squadron, a detachment from Colerne in November 1940. These black-painted machines were night fighters that had been based in the area to defend the Bath and Bristol region from nocturnal attacks by the Luftwaffe. When suitable accommodation was ready the following month, the entire squadron moved to Charmy Down as its first residents.

No. 87 Squadron was to become one of the longest-serving Hurricane night-fighter squadrons. It was originally formed as a fighter squadron during the First World War, as an offshoot of the Central Flying School at Upavon in Wiltshire, and was disbanded at the war's end. Re-formed in 1937 with Hawker Furies, it soon received Gloster Gladiators and specialized in 'tied together' aerobatics at air displays. Re-equipped with Hurricanes in 1938, the squadron went to France in 1940 as part of the Air Component of the British Expeditionary Force. The unit suffered heavy losses during the German invasion that summer and returned to the UK to refit and recuperate.

A preserved Hurricane carrying the markings of the OC of 87 Squadron when it operated from Charmy Down. (Aeroplane)

The squadron saw limited action during the Battle of Britain from its base at Church Fenton in Yorkshire, and towards the end of July sent its B Flight on detachment to Hullavington in Wiltshire and Bibury in Gloucestershire to assist in night-fighter defence. Many contacts were made, and on 7 August the squadron scored its first night victory when Pilot Officer Conely shot down a Heinkel He111. Other flights were then sent on detachment on a rota basis. The squadron's night fighting operations were obviously seen as a success, for in November 1940 it was decided that the whole squadron should go over to night operations and that it should be sent south, thus resulting in the move to Colerne, and then to Charmy Down. The squadron started mounting nightly standing patrols from Charmy Down on the lookout for German bombers. In the new year 87 Squadron started sending detached flights to St Mary's in the Isles of Scilly, on a rotational basis, to defend the islands and local shipping from German intruders. From Charmy Down night defensive patrols continued; then, in March, the squadron began intruder missions of their own, sending Hurricanes over German bases in the Caen area. However the frequency of German night raids meant that the squadron was spending a lot of time in the Bristol Channel area. Contacts were often made, but the resulting combats were inconclusive.

The first success for the squadron while flying from Charmy Down came in early May 1941 when the OC, Squadron Leader Ian 'Widge' Gleed, shot down a Dornier Do17Z. Gleed later led one of the squadron detachments to St Mary's in May and, while operating from there on the 24th, together with Sergeant Thorogood, he shot down a Dornier Do18 flying boat. From then on, the St Mary's detachment more than justified its presence, by shooting down an average of two enemy aircraft per month for the rest of its stay. The squadron continued to fly night patrols over the Bristol and Bath area, and across the Bristol Channel, looking for intruders. Few contacts were made, and most operations were uneventful. On 6 August the squadron moved to Colerne.

On 7 August 1941 two more squadrons arrived at Charmy Down: 125 Squadron with Defiant Mk Is, and 263 with Whirlwind Mk Is. The former had arrived from Colerne, having been re-formed there as a night fighter unit in June 1941. 263 Squadron had flown Gladiators in Norway in 1940, but was withdrawn on the

Defiant NF.I, as flown by 125 Squadron from the station. (Author)

Whirlwinds of 263 Squadron are depicted in this evocative painting by Michael Turner, during the time that they flew from Charmy Down. (M. Turner)

carrier HMS *Glorious*. Unfortunately the *Glorious* was sunk and the squadron's aircraft lost, along with many of the aircrew. The unit was re-formed later in June 1940 as the first squadron on the new Westland Whirlwind twin-engined fighter. It came to Charmy Down from Filton. Both squadrons immediately started operations from Charmy Down: 125 Squadron mounted night patrols, while 263 Squadron flew intruder missions on enemy airfields and also provided escorts for bomber operations. 263 Squadron got off to a good start from its new station in August, destroying three Bf109s, damaging another, and sinking one E-boat and damaging another that month.

On 12 August 1941, twelve of the squadron's Whirlwinds took part in 2 Group Operation 77. This was a deep penetration raid by the group's bomber squadrons into Germany to attack worthwhile targets, with the deliberate intention of also rousing the German fighter squadrons. It was to be the greatest Allied low level attack of the war so far and the first such on Germany. The targets were two huge power stations near Cologne, one at Knapsack and another, nearby at Quadrath, that provided electricity for the German arms factories. They were the largest steam-generating power stations in Europe. Three boxes of six Blenheims (54 in all) and four Fortresses were to comprise the bomber force. They were to be escorted by 263 Squadron's Whirlwinds as far as possible, to the north-western side of Antwerp. Three squadrons of Spitfires were to provide withdrawal cover, while two squadrons of Hampdens and more Fortresses escorted by one Hurricane squadron and 18 Spitfire squadrons were to operate diversions.

All went to plan. The Whirlwinds rendezvoused with the bombers, and the force crossed the Channel one mile north-west of Orfordness, at a height of 100 feet. About three miles from the Dutch coast the fighters climbed to 1,000 feet to deal with any German fighters that were around and give top cover to the Blenheims as they sped inland. When the Whirlwinds reached the limit of their range, four miles north-east of Antwerp, they turned for home and followed the course of the Scheldt, six aircraft flying very low with the other six at 500 feet. Near Walcheren they spotted seven barges, which they attacked, leaving two sinking. On landing Sergeant Jowatts's Whirlwind P6999 was found to have been hit in the tail by an explosive shell, and two others had a number of flak holes in them. Despite heavy flak in the area, the power stations had been located by the low-flying Blenheims and successfully bombed; twelve Blenheims were lost, but both power stations were put out of action for some time.

263 Squadron's last major operation from Charmy Down was on 8 September 1941, providing escorts for a raid on the Channel Islands. They rendezvoused with twelve Blenheims of 88 and 114 Squadrons over Ibsley and with the Spitfires of 118, 234 and 501 Squadrons. The force headed across the Channel towards its target area off Guernsey. There it found two small convoys including tugs towing barges. The Whirlwinds went in first to soften up the naval escort vessels; then the Blenheims successfully attacked the barges. The Spitfire fighter escort was attacked by Bf109Fs, which were beaten off without any claims or losses.

A couple of weeks later a second Whirlwind squadron appeared at the airfield. This was 137 Squadron, which formed at Charmy Down on 20 September from many of 263 Squadron's personnel. This meant that 263 had to stand down from operations in order to take on new pilots. However, 137 Squadron itself got off to a good

The pilots of 137 Squadron gather before three of their Whirlwinds. (Aeroplane)

39

start, and was soon getting ready for operations. One flight was operational by 20 October, and four days later the squadron flew its first mission across the Channel on a Ramrod attack on railway marshalling yards at Landernau in Brittany. Unfortunately, progress was marred when, on 28 October, the squadron's CO, Squadron Leader J. Sample DFC, was killed in a mid-air collision with another aircraft, and when, on the 30th, Flying Officer Clark crashed into the sea during an operation. The squadron came off operations for a short period while it moved away from Charmy Down on transfer to Coltishall on 8 November 1941.

A new fighter squadron arrived at Charmy Down in November 1941. This was 417 Squadron, which was formed at the station on the 27th. Part of the Royal Canadian Air Force, the unit was initially equipped with the Spitfire Mk IIa. It started working up at Charmy Down, and then, on 26th January 1942, it moved to Colerne, where it received the Spitfire Mk Vb before becoming operational on 17 February.

In the meantime, 263 Squadron had remained at Charmy Down, flying convoy escort missions. The Whirlwinds were detached to Warmwell on 19 December, but returned to Charmy Down on Christmas Eve. Operations resumed in the New Year and continued until the end of the month, the squadron then moving to Colerne on 28th January 1942.

With the continued night offensive over Britain by the Luftwaffe during 1941 many ideas were tried to help to intercept the German bombers. One of these was the Turbinlite, an aircraft-mounted searchlight devised by Wing Commander H. Helmore. His plan called for a twin-engined aircraft to carry Airborne Interception (AI) radar, together with a large searchlight called a Turbinlite mounted in the nose. The Turbinlite aircraft would be accompanied by a single-engined interceptor, known as a Satellite. Once the Turbinlite aircraft picked up a contact on its radar, it would close in and illuminate the target. The Satellite would then move in for the kill once the target was positively identified as an enemy aircraft. The concept was developed very quickly, the Douglas Havoc twin-engined fighter (or the bomber version, the Boston) being selected to carry the searchlight and radar. Ten flights of the Turbinlite aircraft were formed, and they were paired with Hurricane night fighter squadrons to put the idea into practice.

Two Turbinlite flights were formed at Colerne: 1454, on 27 June 1941, paired with 87 Squadron; and 1457, on 15 September 1941, to work with 247 Squadron. Fighters were to be made available by the Hurricane squadrons to fly with the Turbinlite aircraft when required. The units started operations, and, although some contacts were made, there were no interceptions. No. 1454 Flight moved with 87 Squadron from Colerne to Charmy Down on 27 January 1942 and regularly sent detachments from there to Exeter. The unit made its first operational flight on 24 March. However, a general problem found with most of the Turbinflite flights was that the Hurricane squadrons they were attached to didn't see them as a priority when it came to other demands on their aircraft. This was solved in September 1942, when the Turbinlite flights were expanded into squadrons, each comprising a flight of Bostons or Havocs and a flight of Hurricanes.

No. 1454 Flight became 533 Squadron on 8 September 1942. Standing patrols were often flown by the unit, depending on the availability of aircraft and aircrew and the weather conditions. In August 1942, for example, 17 patrols were flown, and 21 the following month, but few contacts appeared on the radar. Meanwhile 87 Squadron had continued to fly night patrols of its own, but they too made few contacts. In May 1942 the squadron had begun to mount offensive operations again over the Continent. This continued throughout the summer months, apart from a very brief interlude in August when, on the 19th, 87 Squadron took part in Operation Jubilee. This was a major operation, undertaken to test the feasibility of an amphibious landing on the Continent by mounting a commando raid on Dieppe. A large number of Allied air missions were flown in support of the raid, involving 72 RAF and USAAF fighter and bomber squadrons. No. 87 was one of the eight Hurricane squadrons which supported the Canadian troops making the landings by bombing and strafing German airfields, transport, and installations.

Other squadrons used Charmy Down for forward deployment or detachments. On 23 August 1942, 234 Squadron flew in with its Spitfire Mk Vs, but stayed for only a week or so. Part of the Portreath Wing, it too flew offensive sweeps over France between home defence patrols.

Boston of 107 Squadron that flew from Charmy Down during September 1942.
(Aeroplane)

87 Squadron was given notice to move again in September, this time to North Africa. Personnel started packing kit, stores and equipment, and, on 2 November, the squadron's aircraft took off on the first stage of their journey to Gibraltar. The remaining personnel and equipment left by road to embark aboard a troopship for the Mediterranean. The squadron was subsequently to take part in Operation Torch, the Allied invasion of North Africa, and then provided air cover for the First Army throughout the invasion campaign.

Bomber deployments also took place at Charmy Down. On 8 September 1942 six Bostons of 88 Squadron were on detachment at the station when they flew on 2 Group Ramrod 37 to the Continent. Escorted by Spitfires of the Polish Wing from Northolt, the bombers crossed the Channel at low level for an attack on shipping in Le Havre. They scored two hits on M-class gunboats in the harbour, but as the battle formation turned to come back across the Channel, they were attacked by ten FW190s. The Spitfires of 315 Squadron drove off the German fighters in the ensuing dogfight, without claim or loss to either side. From Charmy Down the Bostons of 107 Squadron later took part in one of the most successful of 2 Group operations of the month when, on 15 September they attacked the *Solghist*, a 12,000 ton warship in the dry docks at Cherbourg. The ship was hit by the Bostons' bombs and burnt out.

Transferring from Middle Wallop, 245 Squadron arrived at Charmy Down on 26 October 1942. This fighter squadron flew the Hurricane IIb and from Charmy Down it continued its task as a home defence squadron, but also took part in offensive sweeps over France. It left on 29 January 1943 for Peterhead.

By late 1942 German night intruder operations had generally declined, and in any case advances in AI radar had rendered the somewhat cumbersome Turbinlite system superfluous. All ten squadrons were disbanded in January 1943, 533 Squadron closing down at Charmy Down on the 25th.

The Fighter Leader School was established at Chedworth on 15 January 1943, and, after completing its first course, moved to Charmy Down on 9 February 1943. Equipped with 36 Spitfire Vs, the school was part of 52 OTU, based at Aston Down. Its task was to mount training courses in tactics for potential fighter unit flight-

and squadron-commanders and also to explore new tactics. As part of the training, front-line pilots were often asked to lecture to the pupils. On one occasion, Wing Commander England and Squadron Leaders Griffiths and Pelly-Fry of 88 Squadron were asked to talk to FLS students about Boston operations. This led to a debate, following which a new tactic for Boston crews in evading enemy fighters was devised by these three skilled pilots. It was based on a corkscrew, but was developed so that when enemy fighters attacked a three-ship Boston formation, the leader would porpoise, whilst the other two performed a rotating corkscrew. The manoeuvre required careful timing, but, with practice, boxes and eventually whole squadrons could perform it, and it was capable of confusing enemy fighter pilots sufficiently to put them off their aim. Trials of the new tactic were mounted at the FLS, and none of the Spitfire pilots was able to get into a satisfactory firing position against aircraft in the Boston formation, despite trying for over half an hour.

It soon became standard practice for one of the Boston squadrons to fly to Charmy Down for the end of each monthly FLS course to exercise with the students. For the purposes of the exercise, the Bristol Channel would represent the English Channel, and the Bostons would cross it. A dozen FLS students would then fly their Spitfires, marked with red tails or spinners to indicate that they were the enemy, against the Bostons, and another two dozen Spitfires, flown by students, would act as friendly fighters. The pilots would then practise escorting, evasion, and interception, returning afterwards to Charmy Down for debriefing and discussion.

Charmy Down suited the FLS well, and the courses that it mounted there were very successful. However, in July 1943 the unit was notified that the station had been allocated to the USAAF and was given notice to move, which it did in early August, to join its parent unit, 52 OTU, at Aston Down. After the FLS's forced move to Aston Down, Charmy Down remained vacant for some time before the Americans took up residence. In the interim it was used for the temporary accommodation of RAF Regiment personnel, over 2,000 of whom stayed at the station during the autumn of 1943.

Charmy Down was transferred to the US Ninth Air Force in November 1943 and was opened by them as Station 487. The first

P-51 Mustangs were repaired and maintained by the 4th Tactical Air Depot. (Author)

unit to be based there was the 4th Tactical Air Depot, the task of which was to repair, store and maintain Alison-engined fighters such as P-38 Lightnings and P-51 Mustangs. However, the activity did not really get underway before it was transferred to Kingston Bagpuize in Oxfordshire early in 1944.

The US Ninth Air Force Service Command maintained staff at Charmy Down, and, on 7 March 1944, the first personnel of a new unit arrived at the station. They were from the 422nd Night Fighter Squadron of the 474th Fighter Group, a unit that was to be equipped with the new Northrop P-61 Black Widow twin-engined night fighter. Charmy Down had been selected as the base for three night-fighter squadrons that were to train on the new P-61 and work up to operational standard before moving to the Continent after the planned invasion later in 1944. As there was no sign of their new fighters, however, the squadron's pilots maintained their flying hours on the unit's Airspeed Oxford and Cessna C-78 Bobcat communications aircraft. They were joined by personnel of the

423rd Night Fighter Squadron on 18 April, and they too kicked their heels while awaiting their P-61s.

At around this time, a Ninth Air Force Troop Carrier Service Wing (Provisional) was established at Charmy Down, to support the USAAF troop carrier squadrons that were based in the South-West. The limited flying that Charmy Down saw during this period included the mounting of clandestine operations by USAAF C-47s to occupied France in support of the OSS and French Resistance groups.

On 6 May, the personnel of the 422nd NFS were moved out and sent to the RAF night-fighter OTU at Scorton in North Yorkshire. There, a few weeks later, they received the first of the P-61s. They trained on these at Scorton and flew their first operational missions from Hurn at the end of June, then returning to Scorton before moving to Normandy a few months later.

In the meantime the 423rd NFS was still waiting for its aircraft at Charmy Down. No more P-61s were available at this stage, but Douglas A-20 Havocs were; so it was decided to re-role the 423rd as a night photographic reconnaissance unit using the A-20 – or the

The 423rd NFS were re-roled with the A-20 Havoc in May 1943. (Aeroplane)

F-3A, as the PR version of the A-20 was designated – and the squadron was transferred to the 10th Photo Reconnaissance Group, based at Chalgrove, south of Oxford. The unit trained with its new aircraft and made its first sorties over the invasion beaches on 6 June 1944.

On 26 May, the third squadron that was originally to have been part of the 474th Fighter Group arrived at Charmy Down. This was the 425th NFS and it too waited for its aircraft at the station, the crews meanwhile flying the communications hacks to keep up their flying hours. However, they did not have to wait as long as their predecessors had for something to develop, as on 12 June they moved out for the RAF night-fighter OTU at Scorton. There they joined the 422nd NFS and started training on the P-61. They were eventually to reach operational status and leave Scorton for Brittany a few months later.

The USAAF retained storage and maintenance facilities at Charmy Down for another few months, but eventually they departed and handed the station back to the RAF in October 1944.

Aircraft were once again seen in the circuit at Charmy Down shortly after the Americans' departure, when the Oxfords of 15 (P)AFU started to use the airfield for training. This was because their base at Castle Combe in Wiltshire was waterlogged owing to the combined effects of heavy rainfall and poor surface drainage. More Oxfords appeared in November, when 3 (P)AFU transferred some of its flying training to Charmy Down, following the closure of its RLG at Bibury in Gloucestershire. The control of Charmy Down and its airspace, however, had once again come under Colerne, and, because of the busy nature of Colerne and its proximity, flying from Charmy Down was restricted, especially at night.

The Oxfords of 15 (P)AFU returned to Castle Combe in early 1945, but 3 (P)AFU continued to use Charmy Down for training into the spring of 1945. With the end of hostilities in Europe in May 1945, 3 (P)AFU withdrew from Charmy Down, and all flying ceased. The station was transferred to the control of South Cerney, and put onto a care and maintenance footing.

In January 1946 Charmy Down was transferred to 54 Group, Flying Training Command and was used for air cadet glider training by 92 Gliding School, which had formed at Yate in January

The control tower remains in place at Charmy Down in 2006, albeit in dilapidated condition. (Author)

1944. The station's accommodation sites were then in use by the RAF as a personnel resettlement centre. Within a matter of months 92 GS was transferred to Colerne, and the resettlement centre disbanded.

Charmy Down was formally closed in October 1946 and was derequisitioned in September 1949. The airfield stood more or less intact for many years after the war, but gradually the site returned to agriculture and the hangars were dismantled and the runways and taxiways broken up. A few buildings remain today, including the control tower and Battle HQ, to bear witness to Charmy Down's past.

4

CULMHEAD
(CHURCH STANTON)

5 miles south-east of Wellington
ST 208154

This station, set in the beautiful Blackdown Hills, was planned as an emergency landing ground and dispersal site as a satellite of RAF Exeter. When it was opened as RAF Church Stanton on 1 August 1941, it was a typical three-runway, A-shaped fighter airfield. A dozen brick twin-bay fighter pens were built off the taxiways, six on the western side of the airfield and six along the eastern edge. A single-storey fighter satellite watch office (or control tower) was built on the northern edge of the airfield, later to be replaced operationally by a larger, two-storey watch office. Ten standard blister hangars were positioned around the perimeter track and later a larger and longer Teesside hangar was built to the north-west. The administration and accommodation sites were positioned to the north of the airfield, though the station accommodation was still being completed during September and October.

By the time Wing Commander J. H. Hill arrived to take over as the first station commander a few days after Church Stanton had opened, the advance parties of the first squadrons to be based there, Nos 302 and 316, were already making themselves at home.

Both units were formed with Polish personnel and became part of the Polish Air Force in exile within the RAF. The squadrons also had names: 302's was *Poznanski* and 316's was *Warszawski*. Both squadrons were equipped with the Hurricane IIb.

The Polish squadrons were soon declared operational and began flying air defence sorties on 1 September 1941. However, 302 was not to fly from Culmhead for long, as on 5 September it moved to Warmwell in Dorset.

The first accident to occur was on 27 October, when one of 316's Hurricanes collided, whilst taxying, with a visiting Hurricane of 87 Squadron. Both aircraft were wrecked, but there were no casualties.

Luftwaffe activity over the South West was limited during the autumn of 1941, and, although they were allocated to the defence of Bristol and Exeter, the pilots of 316 Squadron didn't come across any enemy aircraft. On 1 November 1941 the unit began to convert to the Spitfire Mk VB, and its pilots were keen to see how their new mount performed in action. On the morning of 9 November the squadron took part in its first offensive sweep over northern France, looking for enemy fighters. It returned later that day with two aircraft badly shot up, but their pilots made successful crash

Hurricanes were the first to operate from Church Stanton, with 302 and 316 Squadrons. (Aeroplane)

51

landings without injury. However, the Commanding Officer of 316 Squadron, Squadron Leader Wilczewski, did not return, having been shot down. News was later received that he had been seriously injured but that he was alive and a prisoner of war.

On 26 November AOC-in-C Fighter Command, Air Marshal, Sir William Sholto Douglas visited the station on a tour of inspection, and shortly afterwards, on 2 December the airfield defences, which were manned by the Somerset Light Infantry, too, were inspected and found to be satisfactory. Shortly after this Church Stanton was declared to be self-accounting, and no longer a satellite of Exeter.

A squadron move took place on 12 December 1941, when the advance party of another Polish fighter unit, 306 *Torunski* Squadron, flying the Spitfire Vb, arrived from Speke, to replace 316, which later that day departed for Northolt. 306 Squadron immediately got down to work flying air defence patrols in the area. On 28 December the squadron started to operate from the forward airfield at Bolt Head, and two days later mounted its first sweep over France. One pilot, Flight Lieutenant Zielinski, was lost in combat over the Channel, but the Polish pilots shot down four enemy fighters in the action.

The weather in January 1942 was not very good, and, although some flying was carried out during the middle of the month, it was curtailed by the wet and misty conditions. Operational flying started again towards the end of the month, once the weather had cleared up. Fighter patrols were resumed, mainly over Bristol and Exeter, but no contacts were made with the enemy. Nevertheless, the odd aircraft did get damaged, such as Spitfire AB858, which force-landed at Church Stanton on 25 February 1942, because the pilot had failed to lower the undercarriage!

A new unit had appeared on 15 February, when 02 Detachment of the Royal Aircraft Establishment, Farnborough, commanded by Squadron Leader C.R.J. Hawkins DFC, moved to Church Stanton from Exeter. The purpose of this flight was to mount special trials, such as to investigate the effectiveness of wire-cutting equipment experimentally fitted to bombers in order to cut through barrage-balloon cables. On 24th March, the CO was flying one of the unit's Wellington aircraft, P9210, over Pawlett Hill, near Bridgwater. Here a barrage balloon had been tethered for cable cutting tests. The cable had been marked with flags and the pilot deliberately flew into it, trying to cut it. The Wellington was damaged in the collision, and started to break up. The pilot, who was the sole occupant of the aircraft, parachuted to safety. A week later his promotion to Wing Commander came through!

In early February, four Air Training Corps units were officially affiliated to the station during their visits; these were Wellington, Taunton, Tiverton, and Ilminster squadrons. Fighter operations over the Continent resumed in April 1942, when on the 14th the whole of 306 Squadron flew a sweep over northern France. Unfortunately, two pilots were lost, including the CO, Squadron Leader Wczek.

The government had decreed that the Services should support the 'Dig for Victory' campaign, and grow as much fruit and as many vegetables as they could. The Air Ministry fully supported the scheme and said that all RAF stations should cultivate as much land as practicable. The response to, and results of this, varied but many stations were very successful, especially where they were supported by the local War Agricultural Committee. At Culmhead the digging of fruit and vegetable plots started in April 1942. Cultivation was carried on when personnel could be spared from their duties, and many saw it as an effective recreational activity. The scheme became reasonably successful at the station and contributed a good percentage of the messes' needs.

D Company of the Somerset Light Infantry had taken over the airfield defences in March, and they were assisted by the RAF Police and parties of armed airmen. A ground defence exercise was mounted on 20 April 1942 when the station was attacked by commandoes. They managed to get onto the airfield and, according to the umpires, destroyed or damaged several aircraft, two fuel bowsers and a tender. They killed numerous defenders, with no loss to themselves. No doubt CO Ground Defence had a severe talking to from the station commander after that! As if to emphasize the importance of the ground defence exercise, enemy aircraft appeared over southern Devon and Somerset a few days later. On 26 April the Luftwaffe raided Exeter, and, although they were seen near Church Stanton, they did not attack the airfield. At the time, the pilots of 306 Squadron were busy themselves, on a fighter sweep over northern France. They met enemy opposition, and lost one pilot, Flying Officer Flisnick.

In early May 1942 it was announced that 306 Squadron was to leave Church Stanton, on transfer to Kirton-in-Lindsay. The Poles had enjoyed their stay in the area and were sorry to go, as a spirit of co-operation had been built up between the squadron and station personnel of all ranks. On the day of 306's departure, 3 May 1942, the squadron's pilots took off in their Spitfires at 1300 hours, and formed their aircraft into a large v-formation in sections of three. They dived on the station in salute before circling and flying off to the east. They were followed shortly afterwards by the rear party, who took off in a Harrow of 271 Squadron.

Harrows reappeared in the circuit four days later, and this signalled the arrival of 154 Squadron. The two aircraft brought in the unit's advance party from Duxford, and they were followed by the squadron's Spitfire Vbs. The main ground party arrived later from the railway station. The last aircraft to arrive at Church Stanton that afternoon was a Royal Navy Proctor with engine problems. The pilot managed to bring the aircraft in, but was injured in the resulting crash landing, along with his passenger.

Spitfire Vs flew with several squadrons from Church Stanton between late 1941 and September 1942, including a number of Czech units. (Author)

154 Squadron's stay at Church Stanton was fairly short. It lost a pilot early on, when Sergeant Oliver died as the result of injuries following a crash in his Spitfire at Manaton on Dartmoor, on 8 May. Later in the month, on 30 May, a squadron Spitfire force-landed at Exeter, injuring the pilot. Otherwise the unit's time at Church Stanton was uneventful. It spent its time in training and on flying convoy escort operations over the English Channel without meeting any opposition. 154 Squadron left Church Stanton on 7 June 1942 for Hornchurch and was replaced by 313 Squadron, which flew in from Fairlop the following day. 313 was a Czech squadron, the third to be formed in the RAF just over a year before. At the time of its move to Church Stanton it was commanded by Squadron Leader K. Mrazek and was flying the Spitfire Vb. The squadron immediately went on to convoy escort duties.

This fairly mundane work, which the pilots found tedious, involved slowly flying up and down the south coast between Cornwall and Dorset, looking for enemy activity. Many Merchant and Royal Navy ships moved through this area, hugging the coast to distance themselves from Occupied France as much as possible. Nonetheless, German E-boats and other surface attack craft, often supported by floatplanes, bombers and fighters, would attempt to intercept these vessels and send them to the bottom. The RAF's patrols therefore became a vital protective shield for the convoys. They were so successful that they acted as a deterrent, substantially reducing enemy attacks on Allied shipping in the Channel. This meant, however, that the convoy patrols became rather boring for the RAF fighter pilots, as their very presence meant that they saw little action!

Incidents and accidents did occur, of course, resulting in casualties for the unit. On 15 July Pilot Officer Jerabek was lost after his aircraft went down into the sea 50 miles south of Bolt Head, presumably because of engine failure. Four aircraft were severely damaged in August: Flying Officer Lashka crash-landed his Spitfire Vb at Church Stanton on 17 August; Pilot Officer Stifan crash-landed his Vb at Bolt Head on 20 August; Sergeant Herak crash-landed his Mk Vc at Church Stanton on 26 August; and on 29 August Flight Lieutenant Raba crashed his Vb on the airfield in bad visibility.

An unusual visitor arrived at Church Stanton on 9 September 1942, a Lockheed P-38 twin-engined, twin-boom fighter of the USAAF. It was flown in by Major Hubbard of the 1st Fighter Group, 8th Air Force, on a visit from his base at Ibsley in the New Forest. The aircraft was the first of its type to land at the airfield, and its unusual configuration evoked much interest from the RAF aircrew and ground staff.

On 25 September, 291 Light Anti-Aircraft Regiment Royal Artillery arrived to boost Church Stanton's anti-aircraft defences. A few days later, on 1 October, there were more arrivals in the form of a party from the Army Film Unit. They stayed at the airfield for a few days to film 313 Squadron for 'propaganda purposes', according to the station's records.

There were more movements of ground defence personnel in October. On the 7th, the advance party of 2861 Squadron, RAF Regiment arrived from Llanbedr, followed by the main party a few days later. They were to take over defence of the station from the Somerset Light Infantry, who moved to Yeovil.

The tedium of convoy patrols was relieved for 313 Squadron on 8 October when they deployed to West Malling in Kent for an 11 Group operation. They flew to Debden the following morning, and from there took part in a diversionary sweep off the Dutch coast, while a large force of USAAF B-17s attacked targets in the Lille area. No contacts with the enemy were made by 313's pilots, who returned home to base that evening.

The following day, 312 Squadron, another Czech Spitfire unit, arrived at the station from Harrowbeer. This squadron had been involved in the Dieppe landings two months earlier, during which it had shot down two Do217s, probably destroyed two FW190s, and damaged one of each. The squadrons mounted their first operation together on 14 October, when they flew over northern France. The operation, known as a 'Rhubarb', was a low-level sweep to find ground targets of opportunity which the British fighters would attack with their cannon or machine guns.

Such offensive air operations had been flown by RAF Fighter Command squadrons since early 1941, in order to take the initiative from the Germans and not act merely as a reactive defensive force. Other, similar types of operations were 'Rodeos' (fighter sweeps over enemy territory without bombers) and 'Circuses' (attacks by a small force of bombers with a powerful fighter escort). These operations were designed to provoke the German fighter squadrons into combat or to divert them, and for this reason Luftwaffe fighter bases were often chosen as targets. Another type of operation was the 'Ramrod' (fighter escorted attacks by bomber or fighter-bombers), which were mounted to destroy specific targets. In this way the Allies tried to encourage the Germans to enter into a war of attrition which the Allies hoped to win with their superior industrial capacity – they could replace their losses, certainly of aircraft, much more easily than the Germans could.

On 15 October all available 313 Squadron Spitfires, along with six of 312 Squadron, took off to rendezvous with six Hurricane fighter-bombers (or Hurri-bombers) to attack enemy shipping off Lazardrieux on the north Breton coast. No shipping was seen, but ground targets were attacked along the coast.

Enemy aircraft were observed over Church Stanton on 18 October 1942, but no anti-aircraft fire was put up, and no Spitfires took off to intercept them, as these enemy aircraft were friendly! They were a collection of aircraft that had been captured and repainted in RAF markings so that they could be flown to Allied bases for demonstration purposes. They were flown by 1426 (Enemy Aircraft) Flight and were based at Collyweston in Northamptonshire. 1426 (EA) Flight remained at Church Stanton for a couple of days, giving demonstration flights in the area.

The rest of October and November was a busy time for the two Church Stanton squadrons, by now known as the 'Czech Wing'. On 27 October they carried out a sweep ten miles north of Alderney, but had no contacts. The following day they celebrated the 24th anniversary of the creation of Czechoslovakia with a lunch followed by an attack on shipping off Brittany. They rendezvoused with Hurri-bombers off Start Point, and flew to the Lezardrieux area. Ground targets were then attacked, including railway locomotives.

On 4 November Church Stanton was very busy. As there was no flying that day, it had been arranged that an RAF squadron could transit through. This was 912 Balloon Squadron, consisting of 100 personnel and 47 vehicles. The following day the convoy left again, for Falmouth.

A sweep over the Channel on 3 November and a reconnaissance to the September Isles, north of Brittany, found no enemy activity. Things were different on 7 November, however, when the Czech Wing escorted a daylight USAAF B-17 attack on Brest. Two FW190s attacked the bombers, but were seen off by 312 Squadron's Spitfires. The squadrons escorted more B-17 daylight raids throughout November, on the Bay of Biscay ports, including St Nazaire and Lorient, as well as taking part in more Rhubarbs. Most of these operations went off without incident, but on 18 November, Flight Sergeant H. Louzek's Spitfire was hit by flak west of Lanion after attacking railway locomotives and crashed into the sea.

The Czech Wing took part in fewer operations during December, mainly because of the weather. On 6 December, they flew from Westhampnett on 2 Group Circus 241, acting as top cover for a diversionary raid by USAAF B-24s on Abbeville aerodrome, prior to a USAAF B-17 attack on the locomotive works at Lille. This in turn was a diversion for Operation Oyster, a large 2 Group raid on the Philips radio and valve factory at Eindhoven. The largest German-controlled such factory in Europe, it supplied a third of the Germans' radio valves, as well as important radar components. Of the attacking Venturas, Mitchells, Bostons and Mosquitos, 14 aircraft were lost, but the factory, which was in a densely populated part of the city, was destroyed with only minimal loss of civilian lives.

Spitfire V in flight. (Author)

On 20 December the wing flew on 2 Group Circus 244 in support of 90 B-17s and B-24s returning from a raid on Rouilly airport. Some enemy aircraft were seen, but no contacts were made with them. The last mission before Christmas was on 23 December, when the wing flew close escort to 18 RAF Bostons in an attack on the docks at St Malo.

On 25 December 1942 the traditional RAF Christmas Dinner was held in the new airmen's mess at Church Stanton, the other ranks being served with their meals by the officers and SNCOs. The Czech Wing's last operation for 1942 was on 30 December, when they flew top cover for 70 B-17s which raided the U-boat pens at Lorient. No enemy aircraft were seen.

The first operation of 1943 was 10 Group Rodeo 27 over Brittany on 2 January. Despite (or perhaps because of) a heavy RAF bomber and fighter presence, there was no reaction from the enemy. They flew again the following day on Rodeo 28, 312 and 313 acting as first diversion squadrons, and 310 as secondary, during an attack by 85 B-17s on St Nazaire docks. Once again, no enemy aircraft were encountered. That afternoon 312 and 313 Squadrons flew out again to the French coast to cover the return of the last boxes of B-17s from St Nazaire.

The first losses for 1943 were on 15 January during 10 Group's Circus 13, which was in support of a raid by twelve Bostons on shipping in the dry dock at Cherbourg. No enemy aircraft were seen, but as the formation approached the target, two Spitfires of 313 Squadron collided, killing their pilots, Flying Officer Kratkoruky and Flight Sergeant Blaha.

The three 10 Group Ramrods that followed in January were severely affected by bad weather. Ramrod 49, taking twelve Venturas to raid the railway viaduct at Morlaix was abandoned over the French coast, and the formation turned for home. While over the Channel the Spitfires of 310 and 312 Squadrons were diverted to help deal with six FW190s that were mounting a rhubarb of their own on Dartmouth. As the Spitfires neared the town, they saw one of the FW190s shot down into the sea by a Typhoon that was already on the scene. None of the remaining raiders was seen.

On 21 January a USAAF B-17 landed at Church Stanton with engine trouble. The aircraft was returning from North Africa via

Predannack. Ramrod 49 was repeated (as Ramrod 50) on 29 January, and the Morlaix viaduct was bombed according to plan. The bombers were attacked by ten FW190s as the formation returned over the French coast, but these were driven off by the Spitfires without loss.

Film crews reappeared at the station on 7 February, with the arrival of a unit from Two Cities Films to carry out the flying sequences for the film *Flemish Farm*. The film was set on a Belgian airfield in 1940 and a British one in 1942. Hurricanes from Harrowbeer were flown in for some of the shots. Location shooting with actors Clifford Evans, Clive Brook and Jane Baxter continued over the ensuing ten days, while the station carried on with a gas exercise and the squadron flew two fighter sweeps and two Ramrods to St Malo and St Nazaire!

Enemy aircraft were getting more aggressive at this time. On 19 February Flight Sergeant Valasek was test flying one of 313 Squadron's high-altitude Spitfires when he met two FW190s at 23,000 feet over Newton Abbot. He fired a quick burst of machine gun fire at 500 yards before making his escape. A week later, on 26 February, a section of 313 Squadron aircraft returning from a patrol met eight FW190s that had just bombed Exmouth. Flying Officer Masarik turned to follow, and, although he was not able to close on them, he managed to direct a couple of Rhodesian Typhoons onto their course. The Typhoons shot down two of the German fighters without loss.

More Ramrods followed over the next few months. 10 Group Ramrod 54 on 27 February was one of the more eventful of these. The escorting fighter squadrons assembled at Predannack in Cornwall, later to return to Church Stanton and Bolt Head. The aim of the mission was to provide cover for a B-17 attack on Brest. After take-off and rendezvous with the bombers, the formation was approaching the target from the north when it was attacked by a number of FW190s. Blue Section of 313 Squadron warded off two attacks, but then became separated from the main force. In the ensuing dogfight over Île de Batz, one of the FW190s was hit and severely damaged, but Flight Lieutenant Stasak was shot down.

Other operations during this period included escorting Whirlwind fighter-bombers during attacks on Luftwaffe airfields, and B-24 attacks on Brest. Enemy opposition was now regularly being met on these operations, usually from FW190s. One of 313 Squadron's Spitfires, flown by Pilot Officer Prihoda, was shot down near Brest on 6 March, in return for one damaged FW190, and Flight Sergeant Stefan was shot down while escorting a force of 60 B-17s to Rennes three days later.

Through the rest of March, Ramrods were mixed with convoy escorts and shipping recces (reconnaissance), looking for hostile naval forces. On one of the latter, on 25 March, a section of 313 Squadron Spitfires was attacked by a German standing patrol. Outnumbered, the Czechs headed back across the Channel, but were pursued for 30 miles by the FW190s before the Germans finally gave up.

During April the Church Stanton squadrons took part in nine ramrod-type operations, three Rodeo-type operations, two Circuses and four shipping recces. An example of these operations was,

From 1942 one of the main adversaries for the Church Stanton squadrons was the FW190. (Aeroplane)

61

10 Group Circus 22, on 13 April, which was to escort a Whirlwind attack on Guipavas airfield near Brest. 313 Squadron flew with Portreath Wing for this operation, which went according to plan, without loss. Another typical day during this period was 14 April, when shipping recces were flown in the morning, and in the afternoon sections of 312 and 313 Squadrons' aircraft escorted Supermarine Walruses and Air Sea Rescue launches to locate and pick up the crew of a Lancaster bomber that had ditched 40 miles south of Plymouth. Other aircraft from Church Stanton escorted a Whirlwind attack on enemy shipping off the Breton coast that afternoon.

May started with 312 and 313 Squadrons deploying to Portreath for 10 Group's Circus no. 28. This entailed a massed attack by fighters on Brest prior to a B-17 raid on St Nazaire. The Portreath Wing acted as leading fighter cover at 23,000 feet. The Exeter Wing flew as main cover 2,000 feet above, with the new Spitfire Mk IXs of the Kenley Wing as top cover, at 27,000 feet. A few enemy aircraft were seen, but no combats resulted and the mission went off as planned.

Combat did occur, however, two days later, when 313 Squadron and one flight of 310 Squadron were escorting Whirlwind attacks on the Breton coast. When turning for home north of the Île de Batz, the 310 Squadron flight was attacked by FW190s. One Spitfire was shot down into the sea and another was damaged. Wing Commander Dolezai, CO of 313 Squadron, damaged one of the FW190s.

May 14 was an eventful day. At 0730 hours the stand-by section of 313 Squadron was scrambled to intercept enemy aircraft reported over the South Devon coast. They spotted two contacts over Torquay but couldn't catch them. A section of Typhoons from 193 Squadron, based at Harrowbeer, landed at 0845 hours for refuelling after an attempted interception of two Bf109s spotted near Bolt Head. Later that day the wing flew to Ibsley for 10 Group's Roadstead 2 (a 'Roadstead' was an attack on shipping either at sea or in harbour by fighters or fighter bombers escorted by fighters). The Czech Wing, led by Squadron Leader Vyviral, attacked E-boats and other enemy shipping in St Peter Port harbour, Guernsey. Unfortunately, an aircraft of 313 Squadron flown by Flying Officer Novak was shot down by flak.

More convoy escorts, shipping recces, and sweeps followed. The Czech squadrons flew with 11 Group Circus 301 over Abbeville on 21 May and 10 Group's Roadstead 71 off Cherbourg on 29 May. Later that day they also took part in 10 Group Ramrod 67, flying with a B-17 attack on U-boat pens at St Nazaire and La Pallice.

Shipping recces in June were interspersed with a couple of escort operations and air-sea rescue missions (including the successful pick up of a Spitfire pilot ten miles off the Breton coast on 7 June). On 18 June Church Stanton Spitfires located a missing ASR Walrus in mid-Channel. It had obviously landed and couldn't take off again, and was being towed back to harbour by an ASR launch. The Spitfires circled overhead to deter any enemy aircraft until the launch was in sight of the Devon coast.

The Czech Wing operated from Hornchurch on 22 June when they covered the withdrawal of a large daylight B-17 raid on the Ruhr. Enemy aircraft were met, but air-to-air combats were inconclusive. This was the last mission for the wing from Church Stanton, as it had been decided to move it to Scotland. After eight months at the station, 312 Squadron was the first to depart to Skaebrae. Fourteen Handley Page Harrow transports were flown in to take the squadron's personnel and equipment, and they departed for Scotland on the morning of 24 June. 313 Squadron remained for another few days to perform more missions. The squadron's Spitfires took off later that morning to rendezvous over Warmwell with the Ibsley Wing and twelve Venturas for an attack on Maupertus airfield, a fighter base near Cherbourg. After lunch, 313 moved to Portreath with 310 Squadron, and together they took part in 10 Group Circus 38, involving an attack by twelve Mitchells on Guipavas airfield near Brest. The Czech Wing provided the main escort, while the Portreath Wing flew escort cover, and the Ibsley Wing top cover. Despite accurate and heavy flak over the target, the mission went off successfully. German fighters were encountered on the return, but were engaged by 310 Squadron, whose pilots claimed two FW190s damaged.

312 Squadron had exchanged places with another Spitfire Vb squadron, No. 234, which arrived from Skaebrae on the evening of the 24th. However, they were not to stay long at Church Stanton; under the code name Operation Kaolin, the squadron was ordered to prepare for another move and was withdrawn from frontline

Spitfire IXs were flown by a number of Church Stanton's squadrons. Here is one in its pen about to start up. (Aeroplane)

service with 11 Group. Most of its personnel were to leave within a few weeks for Australia, in order to form the basis of a new Spitfire unit there, No. 549 Squadron in Queensland.

On 28 June it was 313 Squadron's turn to move, after just over twelve months at Church Stanton. The squadron's gear and equipment were packed into Harrow transport aircraft, along with that of 3075 Servicing Echelon, that had been formed to support both Czech squadrons. The transport aircraft and Spitfires took off during the morning and headed north for their new base at Peterhead. Their new role there was to assist 312 Squadron in convoy patrols and the defence of the Scapa Flow anchorage, but also to mount high altitude patrols in their new Spitfire VIIs to counter German photo-reconnaissance patrols.

The silence of the unoccupied airfield after the Czechs' departure was interrupted in the early evening when the first of two new squadrons arrived. This was another Spitfire V unit, 66 Squadron, which had also been based at Skaebrae. The support transports were not on the ground for long before some larger aircraft appeared over the horizon. These were three USAAF four-engined B-17s that had taken part in a raid on St Nazaire. The bombers were low on fuel when their pilots gratefully put down on Church Stanton's main runway. Two days later, the second of the station's new Spitfire units arrived, namely 504 (County of Nottingham) Squadron, an Auxiliary Air Force unit that was previously based at Ibsley. With it came 501 Servicing Echelon, also from Ibsley.

66 Squadron's first operation from Church Stanton took place on 4 July 1943 when, with 131 Squadron from Exeter, it deployed to Portreath. From there the squadrons rendezvoused with other units to take part in 10 Group Rodeo 38, a fighter sweep off Ushant (Île d'Ouessant, Brittany) to protect B-17s returning from a raid on Nantes and La Pallice. On their return to base the Spitfire pilots found a busy scene at Church Stanton. During their absence five Horsa gliders had landed as part of 38 Group's Exercise Needle, and five Whitley glider tugs had been sent to Church Stanton to retrieve them.

504 Squadron flew their first operation from their new base two days later, a convoy escort off Start Point. An FW190 intruder was spotted by one of the Spitfire pilots and it was driven away. Both squadrons then started operating in a similar routine to that of their predecessors, with a series of convoy patrols, sweeps, Circuses, and Ramrods. They were also called in to assist with the occasional air-sea rescue search, as on 13 July. That evening the aircraft of 66 Squadron took off for Predannack. From there they searched the Channel in the area west of Ushant, looking for the crew of a Lancaster that had taken part in a raid the previous night on Turin. Unfortunately, no trace of the crew was found, including the aircraft's captain Wing Commander John Nettleton, who had been awarded the Victoria Cross after a low-level daylight raid on Augsburg in April 1942.

504 Squadron had obviously been singled out for a special operation or deployment, as it was then ordered to undertake aircraft carrier deck-landing practice and low-level flying training. Whatever the operation was, it never materialized, and the squadron returned to convoy escort and fighter offensive duties.

On 25 July, after a period of unfavourable weather, both Church Stanton squadrons flew to Coltishall as a forward base for a mission to cover an attack by Mitchells on the Fokker aircraft factory in Amsterdam. Enemy aircraft were encountered, and 504 Squadron pilots claimed one FW190 probably shot down and one damaged. Unfortunately, Flying Officer Jagger of 504 Squadron failed to return from the mission. Both squadrons flew again that evening, escorting twelve Bostons to Schipol. There was further action on the following day, when 66 and 504 Squadrons escorted twelve Bostons from Martlesham Heath to Courtrai Iwvelghem airfield. As they were leaving the target area, 504 Squadron was attacked by a mixed gaggle of about 20 Bf109s and FW190s which flew through them after the Bostons. The 504 Squadron Spitfires gave chase and one of the German fighters was shot down by Flight Sergeant Wright, with another damaged by Flying Officer Warwick. B Flight commander, Flight Lieutenant McCarthy Jones, who was last seen pursuing two FW190s in Spitfire BM145, failed to return.

Another Church Stanton pilot was lost on 30 July, after an attack by 21 Marauders on Woensdrecht airfield near Antwerp. The escorting Spitfires of 66 Squadron were bounced by FW190s after having left the target area, and, in the ensuing dog-fight, Flying Officer Zuromski was shot down. This was one of the last operations by the unit from Church Stanton, as on 9 August the squadron was moved to Redhill in a rotation of units. 504 Squadron's last operation from Church Stanton was on 12 August, when, in company with 131 Squadron from Exeter acting as escorts to eight Whirlwinds, they made an attack on Brest airfield. Two FW190s were met over the airfield. One was destroyed by Flying Officer Milne of 504 Squadron, and the other was seriously damaged.

Although their squadrons had gone, there was still activity at Church Stanton over the following few weeks. On 19 August twelve USAAF P-47s diverted to the station because of bad weather. Defence exercises were in fact being held at the time, with the local Home Guard attacking the airfield, which was being defended by the RAF Regiment. Station staff went to assist with an aircraft accident on 7 September 1943. Wellington LN379 of 310 Ferry Training Unit, based at RAF Harwell, crashed early that morning near Chard. The Wellington had left RAF Hurn, but had to put down because of a double engine failure (probably caused by contaminated fuel). The crew was recovered; the two injured were taken to Chard Cottage Hospital, while the bodies of the four that died were brought back to the station mortuary.

Ten days later two new Spitfire squadrons arrived at Church Stanton. These were 131 (County of Kent) Squadron from Redhill, along with 3088 Servicing Echelon, and 165 (Ceylon) Squadron, with 3026 Servicing Echelon from Kenley. Both squadrons were in the process of re-equipping with the new Spitfire Mk IX. When the pug-nosed radial-engined FW190 first appeared during the summer of 1941, it was found to be vastly superior to the Spitfire Mk V that most of Fighter Command's day-fighter units were then equipped with. The German fighter was some 20 mph faster than the Spitfire at all altitudes, and the FW190 could out-climb, out-dive and out-roll it. The result was that British fighter losses increased dramatically. The Air Officer Commanding-in-Chief Fighter Command, Air Chief Marshal Sir William Sholto Douglas, called for a fighter that could meet the FW190 on equal or better terms. Coincidentally Rolls-Royce were in the process of boosting the Merlin 45 engine that powered the Spitfire Mk V by introducing a two-stage supercharger. This added some weight and length to the engine, but the resulting Merlin 61 developed almost one third more power than before. It was installed into a Spitfire Mk V fitted with a four-blade propeller to absorb the extra power and it flew just three weeks after the first appearance of the FW190. The new engine resulted in three new versions of the Spitfire: the Mk VII high altitude interceptor, with pressurised cockpit, extended wing tips and a 40% increase in internal fuel tanks; the Mk VIII, with increased internal fuel tanks only; and the Mk IX, which was basically a Mk V with the new engine.

The first of the three to enter service was in fact the Mk IX, and its superior performance was immediately felt in the first engagements with FW190s, on 30 July 1942, when several of the German fighters were downed by the Spitfire IXs of 64 Squadron. As the Mk VII became available, small numbers were issued to some squadrons alongside the Mk IXs, to give them a high-altitude capability. This was to counter the threat of Luftwaffe bombers and reconnaissance aircraft such as the JU86 which were designed with pressurized cabins to fly at some 30,000 feet, well above the ceiling of conventional interceptors.

131 Squadron was only the third squadron to receive the Mark IX, and it started operations on 19 September. No. 165, the fourth RAF Spitfire IX unit, started to receive its new aircraft on

Spitfire IX in flight. (Author)

20 September, and delivery was complete by the month's end. On 22 September 131 Squadron took part in 10 Group Ramrod 83, an attack by twelve Mitchells on Brest, with 165 Squadron and 616 Squadron from Exeter making up the Church Stanton Wing.

By the end of September all three squadrons had re-equipped with the Spitfire IX, and the Church Stanton Wing flew its first operation with the new type on 3 October. This was 10 Group Rodeo 39, a sweep over the Brehat-Morlaix area of Brittany at 24,000 feet, during which no enemy aircraft were seen. Ramrods followed, escorting Bostons and Mitchells. On 15 October, while returning from 10 Group Rodeo 40, a sweep over the Lannion-Lannilis area, the wing was diverted towards Guernsey to assist two Typhoons which were engaged with six enemy fighters while covering an air-sea rescue operation. The enemy aircraft withdrew when the Spitfires appeared.

At the end of October, to reinforce the importance of survival in hostile territory, an escape and evasion exercise was held at Church Stanton for the aircrew. In 'Exercise Homer', as it was called, the 43 pilots that took part were taken out into the countryside by lorry;

they then had to return to the airfield by eluding search parties of the police and Home Guard. By the end of the exercise, 14 pilots managed to avoid the search parties and get back. Of the remainder, 25 were captured by the police and four by the Home Guard.

The weather had a serious effect on flying operations during November and December. Although several Ramrods were mounted in support of Boston and Marauder raids on western France, other missions were cancelled because of rain, fog and snow, and a couple were abandoned in mid-Channel because of poor conditions. On 15 November the Church Stanton squadrons were informed that they were no longer part of Fighter Command, which had been disbanded. They were now part of the Air Defence of Great Britain. Other former units of Fighter Command joined the Second Tactical Air Force to support ground forces in preparation for the planned invasion of the Continent.

One of the more eventful days during this period was 26 November, when in the morning the wing flew on 10 Group Ramrod 107, which was an attack by medium bombers on construction works at Martinvast. The Church Stanton Wing flew at 22,000 feet as main cover for the force. Shortly after crossing the French coast at Barfleur they ran into about 25 FW190s. A massive dogfight then took place, as both opposing formations broke into a melée. One Spitfire, flown by Lieutenant Beane, a Fleet Air Arm pilot of 165 Squadron, was shot down, and two more were damaged, but in return the Spitfires downed two FW190s, probably destroyed another three, and damaged six of the enemy aircraft. 165 Squadron claimed ten of the eleven victories. After lunch, the Church Stanton squadron took part in 10 Group's Ramrod 110, another attack on Martinvast by medium bombers. This was uneventful.

Later in December, it was decided that, because of the number of RAF stations using the prefix *Church*, Church Stanton should be renamed 'Culmhead' to avoid confusion, and 22 December therefore saw the first operation by the Culmhead Wing, on 10 Group Rodeo 55. The wing left at dawn for Hurn, from where it took part in a fighter sweep over the Tricqueville-Caen area, at a height of 24,000 feet. While they orbited, keeping an eye out for enemy fighters, light and medium bombers attacked 'Noball' targets near Dieppe and further north. (Noball was the code name given to V-weapon sites,including not just the launch sites, but also the storage and manufacturing centres.)

Two days later, on Christmas Eve 1943, several patrols were sent up in the morning. One of these spotted FW190s near Plymouth, but was unable to catch them. In the afternoon the wing swept the Cherbourg Peninsula in support of a force of Mitchells and Bostons that was bombing Noball targets near Cherbourg. Although no enemy aircraft were spotted during that mission, later in the day A Flight of 165 Squadron was scrambled from its forward base at Bolt Head to intercept enemy aircraft approaching from the Channel Islands. The Spitfires located them, but, despite a long chase across the Gulf of St Malo and overland, no contact was made.

The wing celebrated the end of 1943 by covering the withdrawal of a large force of US B-17 and B-24 bombers that had attacked targets in the Bordeaux area on 31 December. Spitfire pilots of 165 Squadron spotted five rocket-carrying enemy fighters that were about to attack a B-17 box near the Breton town of Paimpol, and they went on the attack, destroying four of the enemy without loss. Scorers were Squadron Leader Johnston (one FW190), Flying Officer D. Warren (one Bf109) and Pilot Officer Vance (two FW190s).

The first operation of 1944 for the Culmhead Wing, led by Wing Commander D.G. Smallwood, was 10 Group Ramrod 119 on 4 January. The wing patrolled the Cherbourg Peninsula at 22,000 feet, covering Typhoon fighter bombers attacking noball sites. On the following day the squadrons used 45 gallon long-range tanks for the first time, on 10 Group Rodeo 61. They covered the withdrawal of a large force of B-17s returning from targets on the west coast of France. The wing flew some 210 miles from base, to 15 miles north-west of Lorient, where they patrolled for five minutes before covering the withdrawal of a large box of B-17s to mid-Channel. They then picked up some stragglers and escorted them to Portland Bill. No enemy aircraft were seen.

Further sweeps, patrols and Ramrods were carried out over the next few weeks, limited to some extent by the weather. As well as combat fatalities, occasional losses still resulted from accidents. On 20 January Flying Officer Francis of 165 Squadron was killed in his Spitfire when it collided with another aircraft in a landing accident, and on 4 February Warrant Officer Arnold crashed his aircraft on landing. Although he was rescued from the Spitfire and admitted to hospital, he died of his injuries later that day.

Some sweeps took place from forward bases such as Ford and Kenley during February, and the Noball sites attacked included new launch sites that were under construction. The last patrols by the wing were made over Bradwell Bay, at first light on 9 February, before both squadrons were moved to Colerne.

Defence exercises and demonstrations were mounted towards the end of February to prepare station staff for the forthcoming invasion and possible counter-attacks. Demonstrations of fieldcraft and battle drill were given by the RAF Regiment, and on 25 February a full-scale gas exercise was held. Several incidents were set up, which were satisfactorily dealt with by the station's reconnaissance parties and decontamination squads. A few days later, a locally-based US infantry company which had been tasked with reinforcing the station in the event of an emergency carried out an exercise at Culmhead.

On 10 March 1944, 165 Squadron returned to Culmhead for five days. Their aircraft were there to protect a US disembarkation exercise in south-east Devon, which was one of a series of exercises held during the build up of Allied forces for the invasion of the European mainland. As it was obviously of a high-security nature, enemy air reconnaissance had to be prevented. No. 165 Squadron therefore immediately put up air patrols. They flew two more on the following day, but returned to Colerne at last light, as the exercise was completed much earlier than expected.

A VIP visitor arrived at Culmhead on the afternoon of 18 March, when a C-47 Dakota landed carrying General Dwight Eisenhower, the Supreme Allied Commander, European Theatre of Operations. He came on a informal visit to another general in the Taunton area. General Eisenhower was welcomed on landing by the station commander, Wing Commander I.R. Campbell-Orde, before being driven off by staff car. The C-47 was parked, awaiting the general's return the following afternoon.

The next flying occupants of Culmhead arrived in April. First to fly in, on the 7th, was 610 (County of Chester) Squadron, under the command of Squadron Leader Newberry DFC. Another auxiliary squadron, it was equipped with the latest version of the Spitfire,

Spitfire XIV of 610 Squadron. (Aeroplane)

the Mark XIV, which had the more powerful Rolls-Royce Griffon engine, giving it a top speed of almost 400 mph. The unit had moved from Exeter, where it had been since January, and was accompanied by 6610 Servicing Echelon. While the personnel of 610 Squadron were settling in, two more squadrons appeared a few days later (on the 10th) from Weston Zoyland: 286, under the command of Squadron Leader Joyce; and 587, under Squadron Leader Edwards DFC. Both were target facilities squadrons providing target-towing and gun-laying training for anti-aircraft units based at airfields in the South West. They flew a variety of aircraft, including Oxfords, Defiants, Hurricanes, Masters and Martinets. While 286 Squadron departed for Colerne on 20 May, 587 Squadron was to remain until Culmhead closed.

610 Squadron took off on their first operation from Culmhead at 1640 hours on 17 April. This was to act as forward cover for 10 Group Rodeo 114. Unfortunately, because of bad weather, the squadron was recalled shortly after take-off. The squadrons repeated the exercise three days later, for 10 Group Rodeo 116, and,

in far better weather conditions, they reached the French coast and covered the withdrawal of 234 Squadron's Spitfire Vs. No enemy aircraft were encountered, and the aircraft all returned to base safely.

On the afternoon of that day, 20 April 1944, there were new arrivals at Culmhead, namely, the Seafire IIIs of 24 Naval Fighter Wing, that had flown in from Ballyherbert, under the command of Lieutenant Commander N.G. Hallett, DSC. The wing consisted of 887 and 897 Squadrons, and they were moved to Culmhead in order to provide more convoy escort and strike capability at the station. On 22 April 610 Squadron left for a week's armament practice at Fairwood Common range. In their absence four Spitfire Mk VIIs of 131 Squadron were detached from Harrowbeer to provide an air defence standby section.

Meanwhile, for the next few weeks, 24 Naval Fighter Wing flew an intensive round of convoy escorts, and accompanied RAF Typhoons carrying out anti-shipping strikes on hostile vessels in the Channel. One of the concerns for the Seafire pilots during these sorties was that of endurance, and the Seafires had to hold-off during the Typhoon attacks to ensure that they had sufficient fuel for the return flight.

On 1 May 1944 four Seafires of 887 Squadron flew a shipping recce to St Peter Port and along the north Breton coast to St Malo and Lezardrieux. No enemy aircraft were seen and the aircraft returned to base. In the evening the mission was repeated and five E-boats were spotted in the Lez estuary. On the following day four Spitfires of 610 Squadron performed the recce and sighted several enemy merchant ships in the Lez. Later that day, on 10 Group's Roadstead 101, a section of four Spitfires of 610 Squadron provided cover for Typhoon fighter bombers attacking the ships spotted earlier. On 6 May 1944 four Seafires of 887 Squadron took part in Rodeo 128, a fighter sweep to Rennes and Gael airfields. Buildings and flak positions were attacked by the aircraft, which successfully returned to base.

This pattern of activity was to continue over the next few weeks as part of the build up to the invasion. Enemy shipping was targeted, particularly cargo ships that would be carrying military supplies and E-boats that presented a threat to Allied shipping. German airfields were also attacked, to reduce or, it was hoped, remove the Luftwaffe's capability to interfere with Allied shipping and aircraft. Targets of opportunity such as military vehicles and goods trains were also sought in order to generally disrupt the German army's ability to operate in western France.

During this time senior air force personnel were keen to be involved with operations as much as possible. On 9 May Air Vice Marshal Sir Roderick Hill, AOC-in-C ADGB, visited the station with Air Vice Marshal Charles Steele, AOC 10 Group, and other VIPs to speak to the squadron personnel.

Losses were sustained on these operations, as on the day of the AOCs' visit, when Lieutenant Meakin of 897 Squadron was hit by flak during an attack on Vannes airfield and had to force-land north of the airfield. The following day Lieutenant Van Wijk of 894 Squadron had to ditch his aircraft off the Cornish coast during an Instep patrol from Predannack. Another naval pilot, this time from 887 Squadron, was lost on 12 May when Lieutenant King failed to return from Roadstead 105, in which eight Seafires of 887 and 894 Squadrons provided cover for Typhoon attacks on shipping. The Typhoons found and attacked one merchant ship in St Malo harbour. The escorting Seafires followed suit, and then went on to strafe a radio station at Cherbourg. Another eight Seafires took part in a repeat of the morning's operation, but, because of technical troubles, had to return early.

This proved to be the last operation by 24 Naval Air Wing from Culmhead, as notification had come through of its return to Northern Ireland. During its time at Culmhead – just three weeks – the Wing had flown some 400 sorties over Occupied France. On 15 May, the aircraft of 887 and 894 squadrons took off, moved into formation, and headed for Ballyherbert. From Northern Ireland the squadrons embarked aboard HMS *Indefatigable* for operations off Norway, and later provided fighter cover during actions against the German battleship *Tirpitz*.

Following the departure of the Fleet Air Arm squadrons, 610 Squadron continued with patrols, recces and sweeps, moving to Bolt Head for a week to use the south Devon airfield as a forward base. In the afternoon following 610's departure, another fighter squadron arrived, that was in fact returning to the Wing. This was 616 Squadron, another Auxiliary Air Force unit flying the Spitfire VII, that had previously been based at Exeter and later at Fairwood

Common, near Swansea. 616 Squadron started flying operations two days later, with a shipping recce in the Brest area, followed on 22 May 1944 by Rhubarb 255 in the Reimes/Laval area. Three trains were attacked, but one of the attacking Spitfires, flown by Flight Sergeant Prouting, was shot down, becoming 616 Squadron's first loss from Culmhead. Another Rhubarb, 256, in the early morning of the 23rd, resulted in attacks on two trains, one staff car, two lorries and a radar station. Ramrod 131 followed that afternoon, providing an escort to Mitchell bombers attacking Dinard airfield.

24 May was an eventful day at Culmhead. In the morning eight aircraft of 616 Squadron took off to provide fighter cover for several destroyers operating in the Channel. Meanwhile, the personnel and aircraft of 610 Squadron prepared to leave Culmhead after a stay of six weeks at the station, as they had been transferred to Harrowbeer. Their replacements arrived later that morning, in the form of 126 and 131 squadrons, both equipped with the Spitfire IX. 131 had exchanged with 610 Squadron and had come from Harrowbeer. On 27 May the AOC again visited Culmhead to welcome the new units, and 616 Squadron marked the event by mounting a shipping recce to the Morlaix and St Brieuc area.

The following day aircraft of 131 and 616 Squadrons perfomed their first joint operation from Culmhead: Rhubarb 258 over western France. Four Spitfires of 131 Squadron attacked goods trains and gunposts in the Rennes-Laval area, while four aircraft of 616 Squadron went for trains near Dinan. That afternoon aircraft of 126 Squadron also got off the ground, when twelve Spitfires went on a recce to Batz and Ushant. The squadron flew their first Rodeo from Culmhead (no. 151) the following day, sweeping the Gael-Baud area. 616 Squadron also flew that day, four of their aircraft escorting a Dakota carrying VIP passengers.

The weather during the latter half of May had been patchy, resulting in a curtailment of some operations and, over the last two days of the month, a complete cessation of operations. 1 June saw an improvement in conditions, and eight aircraft of 131 Squadron made the most of this by carrying out Rhubarb 265 over Guingamp, Morlaix, and Landernau. They attacked locomotives and a military convoy. One aircraft, flown by Warrant Officer Atkinson, was hit by flak and failed to return. In the evening a second sweep (Rhubarb 266) took 616 Squadron to the same area,

Defiant Target Tugs were flown by 286 and 587 Squadrons from Culmhead. (Aeroplane)

where goods trains, convoys, and a goods marshalling yard were strafed. The weather again clamped down and although several operations were attempted they were curtailed because of rain over the target areas.

On 3 June 1944, at 0545 hours, Flight Lieutenant Wen of 126 Squadron experienced an engine failure just after take-off, but he managed to crash-land on a hillside. Fire broke out, and the Spitfire was wrecked. The pilot was admitted to sick quarters with mild burns and a back injury.

During the preparations for the Normandy invasion, the Culmhead Wing was commanded by Wing Commander Peter Brothers DFC. An Auxiliary Air Force pilot, he flew a Hurricane during the Battle of Britain and was eventually credited with 16 enemy aircraft destroyed, one probable, and three damaged. On 5 June 1944 all station personnel were confined to base, and orders were issued to paint black and white identification stripes around the rear fuselage and around the wings of the Spitfires.

The following morning, D-Day Wing Commander Brothers led 131 Squadron in the first sweep of the day on Rodeo 156. 616 Squadron opened the second sweep and, together, they hit three locomotives, two goods trains, three staff cars and eight military trucks. A sweep on the morning of the 7th by four aircraft of 616 Squadron was also made over Brittany, in the Gael, Vannes, and Kerlin Bastard regions. This was followed by an attack on locomotives, goods trains and military vehicles by 131 Squadron on Rhubarb 273.

Meanwhile, two Spitfires of 126 Squadron carried out a convoy patrol south of Lyme Regis, but one aircraft suffered mechanical failure and had to ditch. Eight aircraft of 616 Squadron then flew in Rodeo 160, damaging three locomotives and attacking seven military lorries and a radar station. In the afternoon eight Spitfires of 131 Squadron carried out Rhubarb 274 over Dol, Rennes and Lamballe, attacking a locomotive and goods train and four military vehicles. The day's operations were completed by eight aircraft of 616 Squadron led by Wing Commander Brothers on Rodeo 164, which attacked and damaged six military trucks.

More sweeps followed over the next few days, including patrols over the invasion beachhead, until bad weather again halted operations on 11 June. One pilot, Flight Lieutenant Grimes of 616 Squadron, returning from Rhubarb 275 on the 10th, had to ditch on the way home. He was located by a Warwick that had been temporarily based at Culmhead to provide air-sea rescue cover. The pilot was picked up by launch and then transferred to Plymouth Hospital, with minor injuries. Later that day, the Warwick developed engine problems itself and had to ditch. The Spitfires of 131 Squadron, returning from a sweep, patrolled over the stricken aircraft until the crew were rescued by launch.

Bad weather on the morning of the 12th resulted in an aborted mission, but the whole wing managed to get off the ground in the afternoon, on Rodeo 169, led by Wing Commander Brothers. They flew across the Channel, heading for the Luftwaffe airfields at Le Mans and Laval. Several enemy aircraft were spotted on the ground at Le Mans, and Warrant Officer Hannah of 131 Squadron damaged two of them. There was more activity at Laval, as warning of the Spitfires' approach had already been given. Several German fighters were taxying out or were already in the air as the

British formations approached. As the Spitfires went in to attack, Flying Officer Parry of 131 Squadron shot down a Bf109 that had just taken off. A second Bf109 was destroyed by Warrant Officer Hart of 616 Squadron, and a third was downed by Flight Lieutenant Harrison of 616, who, unfortunately, was then seen to crash. Flight Lieutenant Cleland attacked and destroyed two FW190s. Although the enemy fighters had been disposed of, there was still danger from the ground, and, as the Spitfires swept the airfield, Flight Lieutenant Moody of 131 Squadron was shot down by flak. Wing Commander Brothers destroyed one FW190 on the ground; two more were destroyed, and three damaged. As they left the area, the Spitfires attacked locomotives and military vehicles on their way back to the coast. Two pilots had problems at this stage: Flight Lieutenant Cleland of 616 Squadron baled out of his damaged aircraft over the sea and was later rescued, while Flying Officer Edwards, finding his Spitfire short of fuel, landed at a forward airstrip in the Allied beachhead near St Mère Église. His aircraft was refuelled from the tanks of a crashed aircraft and he was soon on his way back to Culmhead.

Intensive operations by the Culmhead Wing followed over the next few days as the Allies fought to retain their hold on French soil. Attacks on German troops and road transport were kept up in order to prevent supplies and reinforcements reaching their front lines. Aircraft occasionally needed to put down on forward airstrips to refuel, but the squadrons incurred no further losses. Anti-shipping patrols were also maintained, particularly round the western coast of Brittany and the Channel Islands, to ensure that enemy warships did not attack the invasion fleet. On 18 June, during an early morning patrol by 131 Squadron, merchant vessels and a minesweeper were sighted near Jersey. Two large barges were also spotted, which were attacked. As well as fighter sweeps, the Culmhead squadrons provided escorts to other Allied aircraft, as on 18 June, when they escorted Beaufighters to attack shipping on 10 Group Roadstead 143.

Bad weather restricted operations further into June. For example, on the 23rd, an early morning reconnaissance by 616 Squadron to Cap de la Hague, St Malo and Lezardrieux was carried out successfully, and an enemy vessel sighted. Rhubarb 296 was mounted that afternoon by 16 Spitfires of 131 and 616 Squadrons, but the attack had to be abandoned because of heavy rain along the French coast. However, later that day, nine aircraft of 126 Squadron, armed with 500 lb bombs, moved to Bolt Head for Ramrod 144, an attack on a radar station at Plouquernem. The target was found and attacked successfully. Also that day, two aircraft of 616 Squadron flew a shipping recce to Cap de la Hague, and in the evening four further operations took place. The first was by nine Spitfires of 126 Squadron, which carried out Ramrod 145, a successful bombing attack on a radar station near Lannion, followed by two further shipping recces, each by two aircraft of 616 Squadron. The final event of the day took place at dusk, when eight aircraft of 131 Squadron provided an escort and withdrawal cover for Typhoons of 263 Squadron patrolling Cherbourg.

Operations the following day were interrupted by the weather, but included missions to escort Typhoons to St. Malo on shipping strikes; to escort Halifaxes to bomb noball targets; to carry out armed shipping recces and a rodeo; and to provide escort cover for a straggling Lancaster returning from a bombing mission over France.

This intense pattern of operations continued throughout the rest of June, interrupted from time to time by the weather. No further losses were sustained, although three Spitfires developed mechanical problems over the target but were able to put down on Allied-held airstrips to complete repairs. During June the Culmhead Wing claimed a tally of four enemy aircraft destroyed in the air plus one probable, four on the ground plus five damaged; 38 locomotives, 39 goods wagons, 76 lorries, 33 other vehicles, nine radar stations, and two ships heavily damaged.

July started in much the same way, with a high level of operations, which were sometimes curtailed as a result of bad weather. On 2 July the first aircraft to leave the ground were four Spitfires of 131 Squadron setting out on a recce of the Granville area. They turned back, however, when they reached the weather-bound French coast. Next up were the Spitfires of 126 Squadron, led by Squadron Leader Plegis, departing not on operations but on transfer to Harrowbeer, their six week stay at Culmhead having ended. Early in the afternoon four 616 Squadron aircraft carried out a shipping recce off St Malo, followed by twelve aircraft of 131 Squadron which provided an escort to rocket-armed Typhoons of

263 Squadron operating on 10 Group Ramrod 151, an attack on the power station at Mur de Bretagne. On their return 131's Spitfires destroyed a lorry and goods train east of Guingamp. In the evening Rhubarb 303, a sweep over the St Brieuc area, was carried out by 616 Squadron, and the last operation of the day was a last-light shipping recce off the Channel Islands, St Malo, and Lezardrieux by four Spitfires of 131 Squadron.

From the second week in July, sweeps were made deeper into France, ahead of the advancing Allied armies, operations being flown to Tours, Angers and Saumur. This was made possible by the fitting of external 90-gallon tanks to extend the Spitfires' range. On 12 July the Wing, using Ford as a forward base, flew as escort to Lancasters bombing targets at Vaire, near Paris.

Culmhead was often seen as an unpopular posting because of its location, but it was its location, isolated in the hills of South Somerset, that led to an important milestone in the station's story. It was decided that 616 Squadron should be the first jet fighter squadron in the RAF, and would be issued with the new Gloster Meteor. Culmhead was the ideal place for the unit to train with the new aeroplane in relative secrecy. The first two Meteors arrived at

Meteor FMK1 of 616 Squadron at Culmhead in July 1944. (Aeroplane)

Culmhead on 13 July 1944, amid subdued excitement among the station's staff.

Meanwhile, operations over the Continent continued whenever the weather (which was still atrocious even for a British summer) allowed. The Culmhead Wing worked with the USAAF on 18 July, when, flying from Tangmere as a forward base, they escorted a formation of B-24s to bomb targets east of Caen. The wing returned to Culmhead that afternoon, where they found most of the dispersals occupied by Spitfires of the Harrowbeer Wing, that had landed at Culmhead to refuel after an earlier escort mission. A fighter sweep the following day, as part of Rhubarb 319, sighted about 30 enemy aircraft in the Mayenne area. As the Spitfires approached, the formation broke up, and the British fighters pursued a dozen Bf109s in one group, which headed south. The leading Spitfires, flown by Flying Officer Edwards of 131 Squadron and Pilot Officer Wilson of 616 Squadron, eventually caught up with the rearmost German fighter, a Bf109G, over Alençon, and together they shot it down, but, as the enemy continued due south, the pursuit was called off and the Spitfires returned to base. This was the final operation for 616 Squadron from Culmhead, for on 21 July 1944 the unit left for Manston.

131 Squadron carried on as the remaining Spitfire unit at Culmhead. On 23 July it took part in Rodeo 186, and, despite the marginal weather conditions, it attacked convoys and goods trains near Alençon. Over the following week the weather restricted operations, which included section-strength shipping recces and patrols, a ramrod on 30 July, and cover for a Lancaster raid on the marshalling yards at Joigny on 31 July. Air-sea rescue operations continued in the area, as a number of aircraft had ditched into the Channel during the many operations that were taking place at this time, with the added hazards of hostile fire and bad weather. The Warwick of 282 Squadron which landed at Culmhead on 28 July was one of several air-sea rescue aircraft that used Culmhead as a forward base for these missions.

For 131 Squadron August 1944 began with providing cover for Halifaxes and Lancasters bombing St Pol, and Mosquitos bombing north of Anger, despite the continuing bad weather. On these large daylight raids escorting bombers, three-and-a-half hour sorties became commonplace, and the formations of aircraft could be quite sizeable. Peter Brothers remembered one particular operation with 250 Lancasters under the Spitfires' protection. The Harrowbeer Wing, led by Wing Commander 'Birdy' Bird-Wilson, covered the front half of the formation, while the Culmhead Wing, under Pete Brothers, protected the rear half. The Spitfires of both squadrons were spread along the length of the Lancaster formation, in pairs, with Brothers and his wingman taking up the tail position. Brothers was able to see a good way along the massed formation of aeroplanes, but realized just how large it was when he was speaking to Birdy by radio: at that point Birdy was over the Channel Islands, while he, Pete Brothers, was just leaving the suburbs of Bordeaux!

August 6 was an eventful day for 131 Squadron. In the afternoon, twelve aircraft led by Squadron Leader MacDougal carried out Rodeo 193, a sweep to Vire, Tours, Châteauroux and Blois. On the way out a staff car was attacked north of Châteauroix and a six-wheeled lorry damaged near Blois. On the return journey two Bf109s were sighted near Arzantan, and chased, but were lost in cloud. Two Spitfire pilots who had been separated from the main formation sighted eight FW190s at 2,500 feet, in line abreast. Flying Officer Parry fired a burst at one of the centre aircraft, and the FW190 caught fire as the formation split up; it then exploded and hit the ground near Arzantan. He attacked another enemy aircraft, but without success. The other pilot, Warrant Officer Patton, chased one of the FW190s to the Le Mans area, firing bursts as he went. Strikes were observed on the starboard wing and fuselage, and eventually the German pilot baled out.

More enemy aircraft were encountered the following day, during Rodeo 194 to Tours, Blois and Vire. When the Spitfire formation was ten miles north of Alençon on the return leg, two FW190s were sighted at 10,000 feet. The Spitfires, led by Wing Commander Brothers, chased them, and then encountered another twelve FW190s north of La Flèche. With Squadron Leader Sammy Sampson as wingman, the wing commander set off in pursuit. After eventually catching up with the German fighters, Brothers singled one of them out, and closed in. The German pilot didn't seem very experienced, and made only gentle turns in trying to evade the Spitfire. After a chase down to 250 feet, Brothers got within range and fired a burst of cannon fire. He saw strikes on the cockpit, and then the FW190 went into a dive and hit the ground. Sammy Sampson had attacked a second FW190 and scored hits, so that it too dived into the ground. Two enemy aircraft then attacked Sampson, but he managed to evade them. During the melée Flight Lieutenant Waterhouse chased another FW190 to the west of Vendôme, but the enemy aircraft got away. He turned back and sighted a further 13 FW190s, ten miles south-east of Le Mans, at 4,000 feet. He attacked one, which exploded and crashed near Le Mans. One Spitfire was damaged by flak; six Spitfires landed on the beachhead to refuel, and six returned to base at Culmhead.

On 10 August 1944, 790 Squadron Fleet Air Arm arrived on detachment at Culmhead, commanded by Lieutenant Commander R.P. Demuth. This unit was attached to the Fighter Direction School at Charlton Horethorne, and was equipped with Oxfords and Fireflies.

Because of their longer range, Spitfire VIIs were used for bomber escorts. On 11 August, 131 Squadron flew its longest operation of this type when it escorted Lancasters for a daylight attack on the U-boat pens at La Pallice. The 690 mile round trip took three hours 50 minutes. As this was close to the Mk VII's maximum endurance it meant that there was little surplus fuel to engage enemy fighters

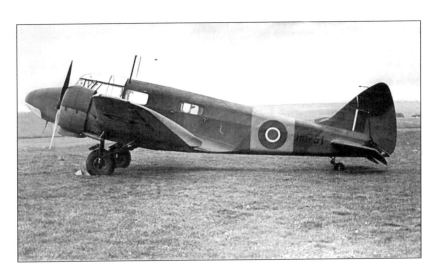

Oxfords were flown by 790 Squadron from Culmhead. (Aeroplane)

that might try to intercept the bombers. The escorts flew above the bombers, hoping that their obvious presence would act as a deterrent to enemy aircraft.

With improved weather, 131 Squadron was able to complete uninterrupted operations for the next week or so, close escorting Lancasters dropping bombs on La Pallice, and Marauders dropping leaflets on northern Brittany, as well as flying sweeps. On 15 August the Spitfires escorted 100 Lancasters bombing Le Culot airfield. For this, the unit took off from Manston and landed at North Weald. The next day, Rodeo 203 was curtailed after eight minutes, when the squadron encountered bad weather, which then set in, preventing flying for the next six days. Intermittent operations followed as the weather allowed, but on 24 August a sweep from Manston was curtailed because of heavy rain and cloud over the Channel. On the return flight to Culmhead the following morning one aircraft, flown by Flight Lieutenant Bearman, was lost. He was leading a section when it ran into a bank of cloud. On the order to climb, his Spitfire was seen to dive into the cloud, crashing near Alderbury. An ambulance and fire

The Spitfire Mk VII was flown from Culmhead by 131 and 616 Squadrons. (Aeroplane)

party despatched from the station found the Spitfire burnt out and buried deeply in the earth. 131 Squadron flew its last operation from Culmhead that afternoon, when eleven aircraft led by Flying Officer Catarall provided cover for Marauders bombing Brest on 10 Group Ramrod 179.

On 27 August the advance part of 131 Squadron moved out, and, after a stay of three months, the main party took off from Culmhead for its new base at Friston. The month ended with more bad weather, and no flying. A few aircraft still landed at Culmhead, mostly visiting, or on diversion. On 3 September a USAAF Dakota landed because of bad weather along its intended route. It was an air ambulance, carrying 14 US walking cases and eight German POW stretcher cases. The US personnel were transferred to the 67th US General Hospital near Taunton and the PoWs and their German nurse went to the 61st US Field Hospital at Merryfield.

Following the departure of the last operational units, Culmhead started to wind down. On 22 September 1944, 587 Squadron was transferred back to Weston Zoyland, and four days later 790 Squadron returned to its former base at Charlton Horethorne. With

Culmhead's control tower seen here in 2006, still in good condition. (Author)

the closure of services such as engineering and air traffic control, the airfield was declared inactive in October.

In December 1944 10 Group Fighter Command transferred Culmhead to 23 Group Transport Command. The station then became a satellite of Stoke Orchard, and a detachment of No. 3 Glider Training School moved in for a few months with its Hotspur training gliders and Master II glider tugs. The unit left again in January 1945 for Exeter, but continued to use Culmhead as a relief landing ground until it transferred to Wellesbourne Mountford in July. The airfield was then taken over by Maintenance Command for use by 67 Maintenance Unit as open storage for vehicles and equipment. This lasted for a year or so, until Culmhead was closed as an RAF station in August 1946.

Culmhead remained government property for many years after the war. A radio listening station was constructed on the airfield as part of the Composite Signal Organization of GCHQ (Government Communications Headquarters). The radio station was closed in 2000, and its buildings now house the Culmhead Business Centre. The airfield itself is privately owned and is used today for flying radio-controlled model aircraft. There is still much remaining at Culmhead. Substantial parts of the runways and taxiways are still in place, as are many of the fighter pens. Several of the airfield buildings still stand, including a blister hangar and the two control towers.

5
LULSGATE BOTTOM
(BROADFIELD DOWN)

6 miles south-west of Bristol
ST 504651

The origins of the airfield at Lulsgate can be traced back to September 1940, when 10 Elementary Flying Training School (EFTS) arrived at Weston-super-Mare from Yatesbury in Wiltshire. Under the command of Squadron Leader T.W. Campbell AFC, the unit was equipped with the Tiger Moth two-seat biplane basic trainer. The squadron leader Campbell decided that he needed more room in which to train his students, and so immediately began to look for a site on which to establish a Relief Landing Ground.

After a careful search, a suitable site was found on Broadfield Down, near the hamlet of Lulsgate Bottom, alongside the A38 Bridgwater to Bristol road. Some 14 acres of land were initially acquired from the owners of Corner Pool Farm and, with only minimal preparations needed, flying started from the new landing ground on 28 September. However, it was found that, because of its altitude (600 feet above sea level) and its location, the airfield had a bad weather record, and so flying training was initially restricted to dual-control only. It was subsequently cleared for solo-trainee flying the following spring.

Facilities at the new airfield were basic, only a few buildings having been constructed initially. Later, two blister hangars were

The Tiger Moths of 10 EFTS were the first aircraft to operate from Lulsgate, when scenes such as that shown in Michael Turner's splendid painting were often repeated. (Michael Turner)

built. By the very nature of Lulsgate as a training airfield, it was not long before the first accident took place. This was on 1 February 1941 when a Tiger Moth flown by trainee pilot Leading Aircraftsman A.E. Joyce stalled while attempting to overshoot, dropped from a height of 30 feet, hit the ground, and then overturned. No one was injured in the accident fortunately. The next pilot to crash flying from Lulsgate would not be so lucky. On 28 March Leading Aircraftsman Villa got his Tiger Moth into a flat spin from which he couldn't recover, and crashed at Long Ashton, sustaining serious injuries.

There were concerns about the security of the airfield, with the result that the construction of pillboxes and defensive anti-aircraft machine gun positions was started in March 1941. Although the Luftwaffe had not shown much of an interest in the Lulsgate area, during a raid on Bristol on 18 November 1940 bombs had landed on the New Inn in the village, killing two of the inhabitants. However, during the night of 16-17 March 1941, German bombers were drawn to the village by a Starfish decoy site that had been constructed at Downside, to the west of the landing ground. The site was located by the bombers at 2130 hours and attacked by them until 0330 hours the following morning with a large number of high explosive bombs and incendiaries. Although some cattle were killed and buildings damaged, no one was killed, which would not have been the case if the bombs had landed on their intended target, the city of Bristol. One of the buildings damaged was Goblin Combe Farm, which was used by the RAF Starfish lighting party.

The Bristol decoys were controlled by K10 Department of the Air Ministry. The HQ for the area was originally at RAF Innsworth, under Flight Lieutenant D.C. Richardson, but later moved to RAF Lulsgate on 9 September 1942. The raiders returned to the area the following month, when on the night of 3–4 April and again on 5–6 April, the Downside Starfish was bombed. Goblin Combe Farm was damaged again on the first raid, and incendiaries and two unexploded bombs landed on the airfield during the second.

Although 10 EFTS, which was part of Flying Training Command, had selected the site and established an airfield there, Fighter Command was looking for new locations for its units. Its staff had decided to develop Lulsgate as a fighter base. Additional land was requisitioned from several surrounding farms to the north, west and south to make an enlarged airfield with three 150 foot wide runways, the main one being 3,900 feet long. 10 EFTS ceased flying from Lulsgate on 10 June 1941, and construction was started the following day on the new aerodrome, which was to be called RAF Broadfield Down. The main contractors, George Wimpey & Co. Ltd, were to build a total of 93 airfields during the Second World War. Work started on the main runway, which runs east-west, on July 2, and it was barely completed before its first, rather unexpected, user arrived. This turned out to be not a British aircraft, for which the runway had been intended, but a German one! Early on the morning of Thursday, 24 July 1941, a twin-engined bomber appeared over the Bristol Channel and flew inland from Weston-super-Mare. It was a Junkers JU88, coded 4D + DL of 3/KG 30 'Adler' that had taken part in a raid on Birkenhead.

89

Having landed on the main runway, the crew brought the aircraft to a halt, stopped its engines, and waited on the tarmac for their road transport to arrive. They were rather surprised to be greeted by the driver of a mechanical digger, who, with great presence of mind, drove his vehicle in front of the bomber to prevent its escape. His colleagues had already raised the alarm, and they were soon joined by members of the King's Own Royal Regiment who were guarding the airfield. The JU88's crew had apparently been victims of the RAF's electronic countermeasures organization, which had transmitted a fake navigational beam from a Meacon beacon near Weston-super-Mare, leading the crew to believe that they were not far from their base at Lanreoc, near Brest. The JU88 was later flown to the Royal Aircraft Establishment at Farnborough, escorted by an RAF Hurricane, to ensure that it was not shot down by friendly fighters! There it was given RAF markings and the serial number EE205 before being transferred to 1426 (Enemy Aircraft) Flight at Collyweston.

The first aircraft to land on Lulsgate's new main runway was a JU88 in July 1941. (Aeroplane)

Work continued on construction of the station during late 1941. By then the main site, which was the administrative and technical heart of the station, was well under way. The station HQ was based around Stone Farm (later to become the Bristol Airport cargo centre). Other buildings nearby were also requisitioned: to the north of the airfield, Clappers, a large country house belonging to a member of the Wills tobacco family, was taken over as the station commander's residence; and a house called Winstones was requisitioned for use as the station sick quarters and had an extension of Seco huts built on its lawn.

On the airfield a taxiway had been constructed all around the perimeter, and on its southern and eastern sides, six double blast pens had been built to house dispersed fighters and included air raid shelters for the crews. As well as hardstandings, six hangars were built (three double and two single blister hangars, and one Bellman). With the two single blisters built on the original landing ground, this made a total of eight hangars.

Although the control tower had not yet been built, and there was no proper airfield lighting, the runways, hangars and technical facilities were substantially complete, and so the new station, under its original name of RAF Lulsgate Bottom, was officially declared operational on Thursday, 15 January 1942. In command was Squadron Leader N.M. Corcos, who had been appointed by

Lysanders were flown by 286 Squadron from Lulsgate. (Author)

10 Group, Fighter Command (situated at Rudloe Manor, near Bath). The domestic facilities, however, were still incomplete, and station personnel had no running water, electricity, or mains drainage in their living areas – considerable privations during the cold winter of 1942!

Although the airfield had been intended for the use of operational fighter squadrons, the first flying residents of RAF Lulsgate Bottom were the members of a target facilities unit, No. 286 Squadron, which arrived on 24 January 1942. Under the command of Squadron Leader 'Dizzy' Allen, this was an anti-aircraft co-operation squadron, whose role was to provide anti-aircraft acquisition and target practice for military units in the South West. The squadron's equipment was mixed, consisting of Lysanders, Hurricanes, Blenheims, Masters and Oxfords. The unit had originally been formed as 10 Group Anti-Aircraft Co-operation (AAC) Flight in January 1941 and achieved squadron status on 17 November that year.

The squadron consisted of an HQ Flight and several detached flights, which moved around the airfields of the South West as required. The author's father, Geoffrey Berryman, served with 286 Squadron, having been with 18 Squadron on Blenheims at Great Massingham during the Battle of Britain. Geoff was posted to the unit at Filton on 9 July 1941, when it was still 10 Group AAC Flight, as a corporal fitter II (airframes) and moved with it to Lulsgate on 24 January 1942.

Airfield defence was initially provided by the Home Guard and by the King's Own Royal Regiment. An anti-aircraft flight was formed on 19 January from RAF personnel equipped with small arms and Bren and Lewis machine guns. They established a Battle HQ on the northern side of the airfield. The joint defence of airfields was not to last much longer, as the Taylor Report of 1941 had resulted in the decision to form the RAF Regiment, the RAF's own ground defence troops, on 6 January 1942. Although C Company, the King's Own Royal Regiment left for St Just in Cornwall in March and was replaced by troops of the Gloucester Regiment, the RAF Regiment was to take over the defence of Lulsgate in due course.

Two days after the arrival of 286 Squadron, No. 3 Detachment 116 Squadron moved in from Colerne. This unit was another specialized one: it was a calibration squadron, whose duties were to carry out radar calibration and predictor checks for anti-aircraft batteries. The squadron had been formed on 17 February 1941, with Lysanders from 1 Anti-Aircraft Calibration Flight at Hatfield. Later equipped with Hurricanes and Blenheims, 116 Squadron moved its HQ to Hendon in April 1942, sending detachments around the country as they were needed.

Building work at Lulsgate took place steadily into 1942, and a major landmark for the residents occurred on 10 February when the NAAFI was opened. Although a watch office and duty pilots' hut had been built alongside the north taxiway to control flying, the lack of lighting and other airfield facilities inhibited operations and so it was decided to move the squadrons to other airfields. On 1 March, the 116 Squadron detachment left for Hendon, and the last members of 286 Squadron left for Colerne two days later. However, their sojourn at Colerne was not to last for long, as the completion of the airfield facilities at Lulsgate during the intervening weeks brought about the return of the unit on 30th April 1942, under their new commanding officer, Squadron Leader M.C.B. Boddington DFC.

Corporal Geoff Berryman did not return with the squadron that day, as he had been sent on a training course to learn about the hydraulics systems of the Lockheed Hudson. This was because 286 Squadron was due to receive the aircraft for target-towing duties. Geoff rejoined the unit at Lulsgate on 4 May 1942, but 286 Squadron never did receive Hudsons! The unit left Lulsgate again, on 26 May, this time for Zeals. Promoted to Sergeant, Geoff Berryman later moved with the squadron's detached flights around its territory, including Weston-super-Mare, Weston Zoyland, and Culmhead. He stayed with the unit until 5 December 1944, when he was posted to 70 (Liberator) Squadron in Italy.

With the departure of 286 Squadron, Lulsgate was transferred from 10 Group Fighter Command to 23 Group Flying Training Command, the formal handover taking place on 1 June 1942. This marked a change of pace for the airfield, as it was then to become a busy flying training station. Together with Long Newnton in Gloucestershire, it became one of two satellites of South Cerney, a grass airfield in Gloucestershire. All were operated by 3 (Pilots) Advanced Flying Unit, which flew Masters and Oxfords, under the

No. 286 Squadron also flew the Hurricane. (Aeroplane)

command of Group Captain N. Carter DFC. The unit was formed in March 1942 from 3 SFTS and consisted of three flights: A and B which undertook flying training during the day, and a night flight. A Flight was re-lettered as J Flight the following year, and the night flight became Z Flight. The detachment commander and chief flying instructor at Lulsgate was Squadron Leader B.E. Moody AFC.

One of the roles of the school was to give refresher training to bomber pilots who were earmarked to instruct at Operational Training Units (OTUs). For communications duties, the unit had three impressed civil aircraft on strength: de Havilland DH80 Puss Moth BM995, DH87 Hornet Moth W9387, and DH Moth Minor W6458.

To enable night flying to take place, a flare path had to be laid out each evening. Originally this consisted of goose-neck flares, which were oil lamps, each with a protruding neck and a wick. The lamps were set out in lines at the end of the main runway, to indicate to landing pilots the approach path to the runway's threshold. The main drawback of goose-neck flares was the time it took to extinguish a line of them when an enemy intruder was approaching. Later the flare path was laid out with portable electric light units. The cables and lamps were deployed from a lorry by the duty electricians, who also set up angle of glide indicators, which were light boxes aligned to show landing pilots the correct angle of approach to take. As with the goose-neck flares, however, the whole lot had to be lifted and re-positioned if the wind changed. As an additional aid, mobile Chance lights – named after the manufacturers, who also made lighthouse equipment – were positioned one at each end of the runway on the left-hand side when viewed from the approach.

Eventually permanent approach and runway lighting was installed on the airfield. This was of the Airfield Lighting Mk II type, which was standardized for all RAF airfields in late 1941. Lights were set out in an outer circle with a diameter of about 6,500 yards (making a circumference of over ten miles), and leading off it was a series of approach lights for each runway; these were in four sections, called the lead-in string, the outer funnel, the intermediate funnel, and the inner funnel, designed to bring an incoming pilot to the centre line of the runway on the final approach. Taxiway lighting was also introduced to ensure that, once on the ground, the pilots could find their way off the runways.

With the expansion of Lulsgate as a training airfield, many extra support staff were needed to service and maintain the aircraft, run the ground training facilities, and provide the administrative and many other activities required to keep the station going. Many WAAFs were posted in to assist, and from August 1942 nearby Winford House, owned by Sir Stafford Cripps' family, was used temporarily until sufficient accommodation was available.

The increased level of flying training at Lulsgate inevitably resulted in an increase in flying accidents. Most were minor, such as heavy landings by over-enthusiastic student pilots keen to get back onto *terra firma*, and resulted in few, if any, injuries. Others, however, were more serious, and some proved fatal. On 22 September 1942, for example, Oxford I W6610 dived into the ground, killing both occupants, Pilot Officer N.L. Casely and Sergeant J.N. Harvey. The aircraft had been flying at a considerable

Oxfords were flown from Lulsgate by 286 Squadron, as well as 3 (P)AFU and 3 FIS(A). (Aeroplane)

height in the early hours of the morning, and it is possible that the pilot misread his altimeter or misjudged his height in the darkness. On 15 October two visiting Fleet Air Arm aircraft collided over the airfield, and crashed into the ground. They were three-seater Fulmars from 761 Squadron, based at Yeovilton, and fortunately each was being flown with just one crew member. One pilot, Squadron Leader Starkey, flying N4008, managed to parachute to safety, but the other, Sub-Lieutenant Shorte, in N4079, died of multiple injuries.

Another spectacular arrival by visiting aircraft occurred late in the afternoon of 23 January 1943, when B-17 Fortress *Thumper* of 360th Bombardment Squadron, 303rd Bombardment Group USAAF crash-landed, ending up on the western edge of the airfield. It was based at Molesworth, Huntingdonshire, and had returned from a raid on Lorient. With their aircraft badly-damaged by flak and fighter attacks, and with no radio or navigational aids, the pilots found Lulsgate in the dusk and advised the crew to bale out before an attempted landing. By this time the aircraft was flying low, and most of the crew were injured on landing, one being killed. However, the B-17 pilots made a successful belly-landing, and there was no resulting fire. Some of the crew were treated in Lulsgate's sick quarters, but the more seriously injured were taken to local hospitals.

A second B-17 arrived at Lulsgate a day or two later to collect those crew members of *Thumper* that were fit to travel and return to Molesworth. For *Thumper*, however, her arrival at Lulsgate marked the end of her last flight. She was dismantled by a working party of the USAAF Air Service Command and taken away by road, to be broken up for salvage.

Group Captain Carter was replaced as CO of 3(P)AFU by Group Captain F.H. Williams on 12 March 1943, and he shortly afterwards visited Lulsgate Bottom to discuss the formation of a new unit at the airfield. This was 1540 Beam Approach Training Flight (BATF), one of many formed to teach pilots the techniques of navigation and landing at night and in bad weather. Beam approach, or blind landing, systems, later to become known as instrument landing systems, had been in use for civil flying since before the war started. They consisted of radio waves sent from a ground transmitter, known by the RAF as a Standard Beam Approach (SBA). In order to land in conditions of limited visibility, a pilot could tune in on his receiving equipment to the correct frequency of the SBA of the airfield that he was heading for and follow the beam down to the runway. Deviations in the signal would enable the pilot to keep on the centre-line of the approach, as well as to maintain the correct altitude and angle of descent. Modified versions of the system were developed as navigational and bombing aids and were used by both sides during the Second World War. The equipment of 1540 BATF consisted initially of eight Airspeed Oxford twin-engined trainers.To indicate their role to other pilots, the aircraft carried a large yellow triangle on the fuselage sides and on the wings. Squadron Leader J.D. Gordon AFC was appointed as commanding officer, and, with SBA systems installed on the airfield, the unit's first course started on 26 May 1943.

Training accidents continued. On 17 May two Oxford Is of 3(P)AFU were seriously damaged when parked ED287 was hit by taxying W6593 piloted by Sergeant C. Dibley.

A brick-built control tower had been constructed in 1942 near the earlier watch office and fire station, but across the north taxiway from them. A new signals square was laid out next to the tower, with circuit and other information symbols positioned on it, alongside the letters LP, which were the airfield's code letters.

Further building took place during 1943 when an expansion of the station was initiated by Flying Training Command. This included the construction in the main communal site of a new gymnasium (subsequently also used as the station chapel, cinema and theatre), a laundry, and a hairdresser's. A living area for WAAFs was built to the north of the communal site, and two accommodation areas for the airmen (Nos. 2 and 3) to the east of that, north of Oatfield Woods. The majority of the buildings on the living sites were huts of various types, including Nissen, Seco, Romney and Laing.

No 3 (P)AFU also flew the Hornet Moth. (Author)

Just after midnight on 2 August, Sergeant R.N.F. Brown was flying Oxford I LX218, which went into a dive. He was not able to pull out, and was killed when the aircraft hit the ground near Quarry Farm, Wrington. A few weeks later, on 23 August, just as Oxford II AB771 was taking off, its pilot failed to correct a swing that had developed. The starboard wing dropped and the aircraft crashed, killing both occupants, Sergeants G.G. Barksy and N.E.M. Williams. There were further minor accidents, including another ground collision, when Oxford I EB738 of 3(P)APU was taxied into by Oxford I LB454 of 1540 BAT Flight. Fortunately, no one was injured in the crash.

Towards the end of September, No 3(P)AFU ceased to use Lulsgate, and transferred its flying to Southrop. It moved out on 27th September, but its place was soon taken by another training unit, 3 Flying Instructors' School (Advanced). The role of this unit was to train experienced pilots to become qualified flying instructors for operational training units. No. 3 FIS(A) had moved in its entirety from two other airfields: its HQ had been at Hullavington and it had also flown from a satellite at Castle Combe. The school was organized into five flights, A to E, and trained its pupils on Miles Master IIs and IIIs, Airspeed Oxford Is and IIs, and North American Harvards. The arrival of 3 FIS(A) at Lulsgate meant that the airfield was no longer a satellite of South Cerney. It became a self-accounting station once again, and the CO of 3 FIS(A), Wing Commander Gosnell, also became the station commander of RAF Lulsgate Bottom as well.

The introduction of SBA at Lulsgate enabled an increasing number of visiting aircraft to use the facility, including those of the British Overseas Aircraft Corporation. BOAC used Whitchurch as one of its wartime bases, and saw Lulsgate as a useful diversion airfield in case of bad weather, shortage of fuel, or congestion at Whitchurch. Ambulance aircraft also used Lulsgate for transferring patients to and from hospitals nearby. Operational diversions continued, and on 31 December 1943 three USAAF B-24 Liberators returning from a mission over Europe landed at Lulsgate because of bad weather.

Training at Lulsgate continued into the New Year, with courses run by the two resident units being well-subscribed. Again, flying training was punctuated with accidents. The first major accident of

1944 to a Lulsgate aircraft was also the first fatal one for 3 FIS(A) while operating from Lulsgate Bottom. On the morning of 15 February, Flying Officer W.R. Rogers flew with his student Flying Officer F. Garvey in Oxford I LW776 from Lulsgate to Whitchurch. Shortly after take-off on the return leg, both engines cut out. A fuel adjustment was made, but the aircraft hit the ground and both occupants were killed. On 12 March the undercarriage of Oxford I V4224 of 1540 BATF collapsed while taxying, but the pilot was unhurt. Oxford DF259 crash-landed on 1 April after loss of power to both engines, but without injury to the crew. Some accidents occurred without the aircraft actually moving. On 9 March Master II DM241 was hit by a contractor's lorry, and on 14 April Oxford V3511 was damaged when its undercarriage was mistakenly retracted at its dispersal. The pilot had meant to select 'flaps up', but, as the flaps and undercarriage levers were so close together in the Oxford, the inevitable happened.

Amongst further flying accidents was a forced landing on 8 May by Master II EM355, following engine failure west of Bleadon, its pilot, Flying Officer T.J. Decourcy, managing to bring the aircraft down without injury. On 12 May Oxford I V3953, flown by Sergeant C.J. Norgrove, overran the runway because of excessive

Harvards were operated from Lulsgate by No 3 FIS(A). (Aeroplane)

Miles Masters were operated by several units from Lulsgate. (Aeroplane)

speed on landing and hit the boundary fence. Another Oxford, Mark II V3862, overran into a hedge on 30 May, while being landed by Flying Officer A.G. Mayfield on the wrong runway in a crosswind in a thunderstorm! A week later, on 6 June 1944, Oxford L6416 crashed near the airfield. It was being flown on circuits by Flying Officer Roots and his student Flying Officer P.M. Cadman, when the port engine and wing caught fire. The aircraft hit the ground, and both crew died in the crash.

An unusual incident involved Master II DM295 on 20 June when the tail unit broke off the fuselage, following the failure of the tail wheel during a heavy landing. Taxying collisions, undercarriage problems, and fuel starvation were the more common causes of accidents, but Lulsgate was a busy place during this time: an indication of the number of aircraft flying from the airfield is given by the fact that, in May 1944, 3 FIS(A) alone had 50 Oxfords and ten Masters on its books. In most cases injuries were not serious, but there were, of course, exceptions. On 21 August Master A2605 crashed into the sea west of Cleveden. The two student pilots aboard, Lieutenant A.J. Hunt RNVR and Sub-Lieutenant D.L. Olds, RNZNVR, were killed.

Diversions to Lulsgate during 1944 included, as well as BOAC aircraft, USAAF Liberators, RAF Wellingtons, and an unusual visitor, a Westland Welkin high altitude fighter. A US Navy Liberator crashed into a wooded hillside at Hazel Manor Farm while trying to locate Lulsgate in the fog on 14 March. There were survivors, although a number of the crew were killed.

The codeword 'Darky' was used by pilots to indicate that they were lost. To assist in the rapid location of lost aircraft, the RAF installed short-range high frequency radios and stations from 1941 onwards. A radio watch was kept, and any aircraft that requested information would then be given a heading for an emergency landing or a course for another destination. Another method of assisting lost pilots was codenamed 'Sandra'. This was a way of showing the direction of the nearest diversion airfield by means of a searchlight. If a pilot was lost he could request searchlight homing by circling near the unit for at least two minutes, firing flares in the colours of the day, and flashing his navigation lights. The searchlight unit would then depress its beam in the direction of the nearest airfield for 30 seconds, then elevate to 45 degrees, and then lower again. This would be done three times in succession, and then the beam would be left in the horizontal position for two minutes. Cones of searchlights could also be illuminated over an airfield to indicate its location to lost pilots.

Two incidents that occurred in the early part of 1945 involved Oxford Is. On 21 January Flight Sergeant K.G. Richards was taxying DF259, when a tractor crossed his path. Fortunately no one was hurt in the resulting collision. Some ten days later Flying Officer W.D.J. Sedgewick and Flying Officer W.F. McElwain were taking off in EB905, when they experienced excessive vibration. They reduced power and brought the aircraft back in for a belly-landing.

1540 BATF still had eight Oxfords on strength in early 1945 and it took these to Weston Zoyland on 6 February, when it was decided that the unit should transfer there. In their stead came the OTU Flight of No. 7 FIS(A), previously based at Upavon, with 13 Oxfords. Flying training at Lulsgate continued uninterrupted until 8 May 1945, when it was announced that the Germans had surrendered and that the war in Europe would end at midnight. The celebrations started that afternoon, and it is not known how many days later flying training re-started! Training did resume, for the war in the Far East was still going strong and trained pilots were still needed. However, a few months later it was decided to reduce the level of flying training, and it was announced that 3 FIS(A) would close on 18 July 1945. Lulsgate was transferred to 7 FIS(A) and became a satellite of RAF Upavon. The aircraft of 3 FIS(A) (now mainly Oxfords and Harvards) were taken on charge by 7 FIS(A), along with the remaining personnel. The Lulsgate detachment of 7 FIS(A) was organized into four flights, lettered A to D, with Wing Commander Chester, the last CO of 3 FIS(A), becoming detachment commander.

Diversions during this time included Spitfires, USAAF Mustangs, and, on 6 September, the first jet aircraft to land at Lulsgate: two Meteors from Colerne that were short of fuel. BOAC continued to use the airfield for diversions.

On 15 September the station held a Battle of Britain air display. There were a number of aircraft in the static park, but because of the weather and low cloud only two flew: a Lancaster and one of the resident Harvards.

The future of the RAF presence at Lulsgate was debated in early 1946. With the availability of airfields increasing as a result of the withdrawal of US forces and the disbandment of RAF squadrons, it was decided to move the 7 FIS(A) detachment to Ramsbury, which had also become a satellite of Upavon. The rundown of the school's facilities at Lulsgate started in February, and at the end of the month its personnel started to disperse. The last flying training course finished on 15 April, and the final packing started. However, the move to Ramsbury was not to take place. This was because in the meantime it had been decided that 7 FIS(A), which had been part of the original Central Flying School when it was at RAF Upavon, should form the basis of a reborn CFS, to be established at RAF Little Rissington in Gloucestershire.

The advance party left for Little Rissington on 24 April, followed on 2 May by the main party with most of the aircraft. The last aircraft to go were half a dozen Harvards. The rear party left for Little Rissington on 7 May 1946, the day that the Central Flying School was officially re-established at its new location. The following day RAF Lulsgate Bottom was reduced to Care and Maintenance, which meant that it was effectively closed, awaiting disposal. For a while the main domestic site was used to accommodate 'Displaced Persons', refugees mainly from Poland and Lithuania. Later the site was redeveloped by the local authority as a housing estate. Lulsgate airfield was used by the Bristol Gliding Club for the next ten years or so, and, in 1948 and 1949, it was also used for motor racing, organized by the Bristol Motor Cycle and Light Car Club, using a circuit of some two miles around the runways and taxiways. The club later moved to Castle Combe.

Lulsgate was sold to Bristol Corporation in 1955 for £55,000 for development as the city's new airport and work started immediately on building airport facilities. The Bristol Gliding Club moved to Nympsfield, and on 1 May 1957 the Duchess of Kent opened Bristol (Lulsgate) Airport.

An extension of the main runway to 7,500 feet was completed in 1963, and the airport facilities were upgraded. The number of passengers using Bristol Airport has grown over the years – there were about four million in 2003 – and the terminal facilities have been upgraded, along with air traffic and instrument landing systems. Both scheduled and charter airlines use the airport.

Do many of the millions of people passing through Lulsgate today realize just how humble were its beginnings not so long ago, or what part it played in the past? There are not many reminders of its time as an RAF station, although until a few years ago one Bellman hangar and a few Maycrete huts were still in use on the airport's north side.

6

MERRYFIELD (ISLE ABBOTS)

4 miles north-west of Ilminster
ST 342186

An area of flat terrain near Ilminster was selected in 1942 by the Air Ministry as the site for a new bomber base. In due course the land was surveyed and, despite the fact that an old canal crossed the area, it was purchased from the owners, the trustees of the Baptist church. Almost immediately, work was started by the main contractors, John Laing and Co., on the construction of a typical bomber base, to be called RAF Isle Abbots.

Three runways were laid, the main one being 6,000 feet long, the secondary runway 4,200 feet, and the tertiary 3,660 feet, and 50 loop-type dispersals were laid out on virtually every side of the airfield. In addition two T2 hangars and airfield operations buildings, including a control (or watch) tower, were erected. A technical site was constructed to the south of the airfield, along with a domestic site. Living areas to accommodate just over 3,200 people were built to the south-east of the airfield, between the village of Ilton and Midges Farm.

Although the old canal that crossed the airfield caused some problems, construction of the station continued steadily into 1943. No. 70 Group RAF assumed responsibility for the embryonic RAF Isle Abbots in April 1943, but by then it had been decided to develop it as a base for the USAAF, which was short of operational stations in southern England. It was one of 16 airfields to be made available to the USAAF in order to accommodate a number of troop carrier groups that were due to be brought to the UK.

The new airfield was renamed Merryfield in September 1943 and was to be operated by the RAF on behalf of the USAAF. By early 1944, the airfield was substantially complete, although it would be some time before the runways would actually be finished. Nonetheless, it was opened as RAF Merryfield on 12 February 1944, when Flying Officer Smyth and a party of 26 airmen arrived from Weston Zoyland. They took charge of the consignments of stores, bedding, furniture, and coal and coke that arrived over the following ten days.

The first aircraft to land at the new airfield was a Beaufighter Mk 10 of the 304 Ferry Trials Unit, based at Melton Mowbray. The aircraft was being flown by pilot Flight Sergeant McDowall and navigator Sergeant Cooper on a fuel consumption test, but had put down at Merryfield when the aircraft's port engine developed a problem. The Beaufighter landed on the secondary (north–south) runway, which was unfinished at the time, having no top dressing. As the aircraft taxied towards the watch office, one of its tyres burst and it was secured where it stood. The aircraft was repaired and it left again on 24 February. The previous day had been a big occasion for the new Mechanical Transport Section when 50 bicycles arrived as station transport!

The next aircraft to arrive at Merryfield, on 2 March 1944, was another diversion, Mosquito HX981 from Lasham, piloted by Squadron Leader Wellington with Flying Officer Baker as navigator. The aircraft landed on the east-west runway, following engine trouble, but the pilot realized that the runway was incomplete only when he was committed to landing and noticed vehicles and workmen scattering in all directions! He managed to land without hitting anything (or anyone), and taxied to a hardstanding. Following an examination of the aircraft, it was decided that an engine change was needed. A replacement engine was eventually sent, but the stranded fighter-bomber was not able to return to base until 10 April.

More diversions followed. On 14 March Flight Sergeant Thomas of 286 Squadron landed in Hurricane KW899 because of bad weather; he took off again later in the day when conditions had improved. On 24 March the first USAAF aircraft landed at

Merryfield, although this also was unscheduled. The Oxford of the 313th Transport Squadron from RAF Grove landed and taxied to the hangar. Its pilot, Lieutenant Douglas Marrs, requested directions to RAF Culmhead. Unfortunately, he couldn't start the port engine again, and so had to stay overnight.

A few days later, the sound of aero-engines and gunfire was heard overhead, and the station was informed that a JU88 had been shot down three miles away by British night fighters. Armed personnel were requested to search the area, as, although one member of the German bomber's crew had surrendered to local fire brigade personnel, three more remained at large. By daylight the following morning two more crew members had been captured and the fourth was found dead.

More diversions came on 14 April, when a USAAF P-47 Thunderbolt landed because of bad weather, and the following day, when ten more P-47s arrived for the same reason. The next day three C-47s of the USAAF's Troop Carrier Command arrived at Merryfield.

These aircraft were in fact the first scheduled arrivals at the station, as they contained officers of the IXth Troop Carrier Command (TCC) of the US Ninth Air Force, who had come to inspect the station as the new home for one of their troop carrier wings. The inspection obviously went well, as over the next couple of weeks there was a gradual move of personnel into the station. The first arrivals were in fact from the RAF. They were the advance parties of 2815 and 2892 RAF Regiment Field Squadrons, which had been given responsibility for the defence of the station, taking over from the Ilchester Home Guard, which had acted in this capacity since mid-March. On 21 April, 174 officers and men of the US Army engineers arrived at Merryfield to undertake construction work on the airfield, including the laying of Pierced-Steel Planking (PSP) alongside the main runway. This was temporary decking designed to take the weight of aeroplanes so that the dispersal areas could be enlarged.

From 24 to 27 April a steady stream of aircraft and vehicles arrived at Merryfield to bring the four squadrons (the 99th, 100th, 301st and 300th Troop Carrier Squadrons) of the 441st Troop Carrier Group (TCG), 50th Troop Carrier Wing (TCW) of the IXth TCC. From its previous base at Langar, Nottinghamshire, the group

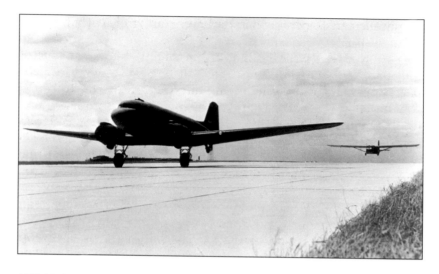

USSAF C-47s taking off with CG-4A glider in tow. (Aeroplane)

brought over 70 C-47 Dakotas to Merryfield, along with a similar number of CG-4A Hadrian gliders.

Soon the airfield was buzzing with activity, as the squadrons flew familiarization sorties around the local area. They soon got down to training for what were to be the D-Day airborne operations. One of the activities that they practised was glider-snatching, a technique devised by US forces in Burma for recovering serviceable gliders from landing sites so that they could be used again. The procedure, which was further developed by both the USAAF and the RAF, involved suspending the glider towrope between two poles so that it could be picked up by a hook attached to a low-flying tug aircraft to lift the glider off the ground. Some of the momentum was absorbed by a steel cable running from a drum in the tug aircraft to the hook, which in turn eased the strain on the glider. The squadrons also practised formation flying, and on 6 May, as well as glider snatching, they flew a formation of 63 aircraft.

On 10 May a busy night flying programme was arranged, and this activity was to become a regular feature of the training programme. In the event, the aircraft of the 50th TCW were to mount their first operations in darkness during the early hours of D-Day.

While the C-47s were flying on the night of 10 May, 900 troops of the 101st Airborne Division arrived at Merryfield. A further 600 paratroopers arrived the following day. Merryfield was to be the American troops' forward base for the invasion of Normandy, and, for the following three or four weeks, they were accommodated in a large tented camp that had been erected on the airfield. The US Army aircrews and paratroops took part in intensive parachute and glider training during this time, usually at wing or group level, but sometimes other groups would be involved, such as the 441st TCG, based at RAF Exeter. On these occasions almost 150 aircraft would fly together in formation.

As the momentum of training increased during May, the group got its procedures off to a fine art, so that it was able to marshall its tugs and gliders on the runways in such a way that rapid hook-ups were achieved. This resulted in a quick succession of take-offs and enabled the group to assemble its formations in minimum time. After practising formation flying, the squadrons would drop their paratroops onto a pre-selected training drop zone, or sometimes over the airfield. The gliders would usually be brought back to Merryfield, where they were released to land on the grass beside the runways. After the gliders had landed, the C-47s would return and fly past the control tower one at a time, dropping their tow-rope onto the ground for retrieval by the ground staff.

The invasion of Normandy, Operation Overlord, was planned for early June 1944. The 441st TCG was part of a force of 24,000 paratroopers and glider-borne troops of the British 6th Airborne Division and the US 82nd and 101st Airborne Divisions that were to take part in the initial assault phase of Overlord, code-named 'Neptune', which called for the Americans to make their first paratroop drops on the night of 5-6 June. The 82nd Airborne Division's drop was code-named 'Boston', and that of the 101st was 'Albany'. These were to be followed later that day by four massed glider landings: 'Detroit' by the 82nd and 'Chicago' by the 101st at dawn, and then 'Elmira' by the 82nd and 'Keokuk' by the 101st at dusk. At dawn on D+1, 7 June, there were to be two more glider landings – 'Galveston' and 'Hackensach', both by the 82nd – followed later that morning by resupply parachute drops,

C-47s were operated by the IXth TCG from Merryfield. (Author)

code-named 'Freeport' for the 82nd and 'Memphis' for 101st. The 441st TCG was to take in elements of the 101st and also glider-borne elements of the 82nd on D+1.

At Merryfield the troops, ground crews, and aircrews waited impatiently, as they knew that something big was about to happen. Their impatience turned to frustration on 30 May when the heatwave that most of Britain was enjoying turned overnight into torrential rain and violent thunderstorms. Operation Overlord was originally scheduled to start on the night of 4–5 June, but because of the weather it was postponed. Due to the combination of winds and tides on the landing beaches, the window for operation was small, and so when the meteorologists predicted an improvement in the weather, the Supreme Commander, General Dwight Eisenhower, made the decision to go on the night of 5/6 June.

On 5 June all personnel were confined to camp and were briefed on the operations that were about to be mounted, as a fleet of almost 5,000 Allied ships put to sea. Minesweepers swept the way for the fleet of battleships, cruisers, destroyers, landing ships, supply ships, and other craft to pass through the German minefields. The fleet making up the greatest amphibious assault ever launched was anchored off the French coast waiting for dawn on 6 June, while that night, at 22 airfields across southern England, the troops and aircrews climbed aboard the 1,200 transport aircraft and 700 gliders that awaited.

At Merryfield in the early hours of 6 June, 144 aero-engines burst into life across the airfield as the C-47s of the 441st TCG were started up. Pilots checked their instruments and did their pre-flight checks. The first aircraft to move forward for take-off was the C-47 flown by Colonel Theodore G. Kershaw, the CO of the 441st TCG. The aircraft gained speed and headed down the runway in the dark, the only illumination being the blue formation light on the C-47's tail. As the aircraft lifted off it was followed by the others, and soon the entire group was circling over Merryfield, its aircraft gradually moving into position in a large formation that would take them to France.

As the squadrons of the 441st TCG flew towards Normandy, they became part of a huge US air armada that was almost 300 miles long. They were formed into serials of aircraft, in five groups of nine, each of three vees. The aircraft were 100 feet apart from wing tip to wing tip (the C-47 had a wingspan of 95 feet), and each group was 1,000 feet away from the next. The formations crossed the Channel at an altitude of 500 feet to avoid German radar detection, flying south-westwards towards the Channel Islands, before climbing to 1,500 feet to avoid ack-ack fire from German batteries on the islands. On crossing the French coast to the west of their objectives, the C-47s dropped to 600 feet, the optimum dropping height to allow the paratroops' parachutes to deploy while giving them minimum exposure to ground fire before landing.

The US Airborne forces had the task of securing the right (western) flank of the Allied beachhead, landing on the Cotentin peninsula behind the westernmost US beach. The area behind Utah had been flooded by the Germans as a defensive measure, and consisted of a marshy area a mile wide and ten miles long. The area was crossed by four causeways, and further inland the flooded valleys of the rivers Merderet and Douve were crossed by two bridges. The 101st Airborne Division were to capture the causeways, and the 82nd Airborne Division to secure the bridges, to allow US forces to exit from Utah beach and get inland.

The first paratroops on the ground were the pathfinders, who landed at 0015 hours, and proceeded to locate and mark four Drop

C-47s lined up ready for take-off. (Roger Day)

Zones (DZ) for the paras and a Landing Zone (LZ) for the gliders. They had to work fast, for an hour later the main force of 800 transport aircraft, mainly C-47s, appeared over the coastline, carrying the 13,000 men of the two US airborne divisions. A precision drop was called for, but unfortunately this didn't happen.

Just after landfall, the formations went into a layer of cloud, which greatly reduced visibility. The pilots instinctively widened their formations to avoid the risk of collision, but, on emerging from the cloud after a few minutes, they had become separated and many lost contact with each other. At this point, to add to the confusion, they were illuminated by German searchlights, and then tracer and exploding shells filled the sky. One of the pilots, Sidney Ulan of the 99th TCS, was chewing gum and said later that the saliva in his mouth completely dried up from the fright. He flew on, but it seemed impossible to him that they could pass through the wall of fire without getting shot down. The pilots were supposed to maintain a speed of 90 mph or less in straight and level flight at the specified height of 600 feet, in order to drop their paratroops effectively. However, many naturally reacted to the ground fire by speeding up and taking avoiding action. In the maelstrom of fire, they dropped their paratroopers as best they could when they thought they were near the Drop Zones. The skies over the DZs seemed to be full of tracers, explosions and parachutes. Almost every aircraft in the formation was hit by ground fire and was unable to maintain height. Several aircraft missed their DZs, and their pilots courageously turned them around to rejoin the stream. Aboard one C-47 of the 100th TCS, Assistant Jumpmaster Sergeant Charles Bortzfield was standing near the door, passing information to the rest of the crew by intercom. The green light above the door came on to indicate that the paratroops were over the DZ and should jump. Simultaneously, Bortzfield and the paratrooper standing with him in the doorway were hit. 'Are you hit?' the paratrooper asked. 'Yes, I think so,' replied Bortzfield as he fell to his knees. 'Me too,' said the paratrooper as he jumped out of the door.

Inevitably, the landing force was scattered, with some 75% of the paratroopers dropped well away from their objectives. Confusion reigned amongst the newly-arrived Allied ground forces, and soon groups of lost US paratroops were wandering the fields of Normandy, looking for their comrades and their objectives. Fortunately confusion reigned on the German side as well, as the defenders couldn't make out how many paratroops had landed, where they were concentrated, and what their targets were. Eventually the CO of the 101st, Major General Maxwell Taylor, managed to rally 1,000 of his men, one sixth of his force, and secured the causeways.

The 82nd found that their Drop Zones had been flooded and remained waterlogged. They struggled free of the area and managed to form up in small groups. Later that morning they were to secure the bridges that were their objectives and to drive the Germans out of the first French village to be liberated by the Allies, St Mère Église.

Many aircraft of the 441st TCG had been hit, and a couple had been brought down over the Drop Zones. Some aircraft did not manage to make it back to base, but were able to make emergency landings at other British airfields. Sergeant Bortzfield's aircraft, for example, landed as soon as possible, with its port engine shot up and no hydraulic pressure. The wounded sergeant was taken off the aircraft on the runway and rushed to hospital.

At 0700 hours on D+1, 50 C-47s of the 441st TCG took off from Merryfield towing Waco gliders. The gliders carried troops and equipment to reinforce the airheads that had been established around the DZs and LZs in Normandy in an effort to hold the area and to prevent the Germans from interfering with the beachhead. More aircraft took off from Merryfield that afternoon on a re-supply mission, to drop ammunition, rations and equipment to the paratroops on the ground.

During the first two days of the D-Day operation, the 441st TCG lost three C-47s and two CG-4A gliders. For its part in Operation Neptune the group was awarded a Distinguished Unit Citation.

Re-supply missions to the beachhead continued. As soon as rudimentary airstrips became available in Normandy, they were used for the delivery of stores and equipment, and for the evacuation of casualties, some of which were brought back to Merryfield to be treated in hospitals nearby.

On 30 June, construction started at Merryfield on a field hospital by B Company, First Battalion of the 1306th US Engineering Regiment. Bad weather hampered work, but the hospital was completed on 10 July, as 61st Field Hospital, and personnel from 813th Air Evacuation Squadron arrived to staff it.

The hospital's first casualties were received on 13 July, when 174 stretcher cases were brought by C-47 from Normandy. Some were taken onto the wards for treatment, while others went to local hospitals. The arrival of injured was sporadic to start with: on 15 July, for instance, 24 stretcher cases arrived, but, three days later, 400 wounded were received. Despite the number of casualties returning to Merryfield and other airfields in the UK, the casualty rate sustained during the D-Day operations was a lot lower than had been feared by the military planners. It was therefore felt that the time was right to assign some of the USAAF airborne units onto other operations.

On 17 July three squadrons of the 441st TCG (the 99th, 100th and 300th TCS) took off with 50 tugs and gliders loaded with ground crews and support equipment. They were heading for Grosseto air base in Italy, to take part in Operation Dragoon, the invasion of southern France.

In their absence the 301st TCS remained active. Airborne training at Merryfield continued, and on 28 July a large exercise practising

Casualties arrived on USAAF C-47. (Roger Day)

glider towing was held with other squadrons. In addition, there were regular services taking supplies to the Normandy beaches and returning with casualties until, on 7 August, the 301st moved temporarily to Ramsbury in Wiltshire, which was used as a centralized freight airhead for the US squadrons that had remained behind from the Exeter, Upottery and Weston Zoyland-based groups.

Shortly after the 99th, 100th and 300th TCSs had returned from southern France to join the 301st TCS at Merryfield on 24 August, it was announced by the USAAF that the whole of the 50th TCW would be moving to France, in support of the advancing Allied armies. The 441st was to be one of the two groups to go first. The units immediately started to prepare for the move, and the first parties to leave, the headquarters element, departed from Merryfield on 8 September. The station remained under IX TCG's control for another two months or so after their departure and was used for the movement of freight and personnel by other C-47 units. The USAAF finally handed Merryfield back to the RAF at the end of November 1944, ending the airfield's association with the Ninth Air Force.

Merryfield was then taken over by 47 Group, RAF Transport Command, and shortly afterwards the advance parties and personnel of several new units arrived: 238 Squadron, 1315 Flight, and 4238 Servicing Echelon. 238 Squadron had been a fighter squadron, flying Spitfire IXs in Italy. Having been disbanded on 31 October 1944, it was re-formed at Merryfield on 1 December as a transport squadron, intended to fly Albermarles. In the event the unit was allocated Dakota IVs, and the first three aircraft were collected by squadron pilots from 5 MU at Kemble on 4 January 1945. 1315 (Transport) Flight was officially formed at Merryfield on 1 January 1945 from aircrews that had been flying Wellington transports with 232 Squadron at Stoney Cross. The crews of both units started conversion training onto the Dakota on 8 January, shortly after the tenth aircraft had been delivered to Merryfield. Over the next few weeks, they were joined by several crews from another newly-formed transport squadron, 243 Squadron, detached for Dakota training.

Towards the end of January, the CO of 238 Squadron was informed that his squadron had been assigned for overseas service, to reinforce 229 Group in India, and was to be raised to a full establishment of 48 crews. The personnel of 243 Squadron and 1315 (Transport) Flight were also to go overseas, to become part of 300 Transport Wing in Australia. A reshuffle of aircrews then took place, as there were several Australian crews on 238 Squadron. The ground crews were also to be split up for posting to the two locations.

The aircrews continued with their training, but during January only twelve days and two nights were suitable for flying because of the adverse weather. Conditions improved in February as work centred on the final training and despatch of 238 Squadron's aircrews and ground staff to RAF St Mawgan in preparation for their move to India. Priority on Dakota aircraft was therefore given to 238 Squadron, until 16 February when there were sufficient crews qualified to fly solo on type to enable 15 aircraft to be allocated to train the crews of 243 Squadron and 1315 Flight. By 17 February two flights of 238 Squadron had left Merryfield and the rest of the squadron aircrews and ground crews followed within a couple of days. The first wave of ten Dakotas left for India on 14 February, and shortly after arrival the squadron undertook supply-dropping and casualty evacuation missions over Burma.

Other visiting aircraft appeared at Merryfield. On 19 February Stirling LK1174 was forced to land at the airfield because of bad weather. The aircraft was en route from Maison Blanche to St Mawgan and was returning empty, as it was to be broken up.

Training crew resumed towards the end of February and included cross-country and medium distance navigational flights. On 24 February Flying Officer MacKay was flying Dakota KJ987over South Wales when he radioed that he had seen SOS flares at sea and was circling a vessel that appeared to be in distress. A Catalina flying boat and a lifeboat were despatched to the area and the vessel (later found to be a Welsh fishing vessel overdue by five days) was towed in to Aberystwyth. The crews of 243 Squadron and 1315 Flight were fully trained by the end of February, and in early March they were sent off on leave before reporting to the personnel despatch centre at Morecombe to embark aboard a troop ship for Australia.

Dakotas were flown by the RAF's 187, 238 and 525 squadrons from Merryfield. (Author)

In place of 238 Squadron, the first crews of 187 Squadron had been arriving at Merryfield. The squadron was officially re-formed there on 1 February 1945 to fly Halifax transports on trooping flights to India. Thirty trained aircrews arrived at the station during March, with the intention of starting operations on 1 April. This was put back to 1 May, as, although a number of Halifaxes were available, the decision had been made to convert the squadron to Dakotas.

In the meantime the Halifax Development Flight had arrived at Merryfield, transferred from Homsley South to be allocated with 187 Squadron for servicing. The HDF undertook the only operational flying from Merryfield in March, using its Halifaxes to operate services to India taking passengers and freight. On 16 March Halifax NA679, captained by Flight Lieutenant P. Wilson, departed for Mauripur via RAF Lyneham, returning a week later. Likewise, on 21 March, LW548, captained by Pilot Officer Kendall, departed for Mauripur via Lyneham.

Flying by 187 Squadron's Dakotas was restricted during March to local and cross-country training flights, but at the end of the month it was decided to undertake some long-distance training. On 30 March three Dakotas of the squadron – KN238 (captained by

The Halifax Development Flight used Merryfield in the spring of 1945. (Aeroplane)

Flying Officer Rotherley), KN286 (Flight Lieutenant Will) and KN154 (Flight Lieutenant Penney) – each with a spare crew, flew to RAF Lyneham for a full route briefing. They then set off to Poona in India, to give the crews experience of the route and the airfields that they would be using. Prior to the start of route-flying, other Dakotas from the squadron were returned to 5 MU at Kemble to be fitted with passenger seats and other equipment, in preparation for their new long-distance trooping role. To support the new services, briefing, passenger and freight sections, together with transit accommodation, were set up at Merryfield to deal with the influx of passengers and crews that were expected.

At the end of the month 187 Squadron had 17 Dakotas and 25 Halifaxes on strength, the HDF had three Halifaxes and the station flight had one Oxford and one Proctor.

Visiting aircraft during March included several C-47s of the US 31st Troop Carrier Group. They flew in from airfields A42 and A61 on the Continent to collect casualties from the field hospital and take them to Renfrew. They then returned to base at Grave.

On 1 April 1945 Dakota KN292, captained by Squadron Leader Thirwell, took off with freight on a training flight to India. The established route was Merryfield – Elmas – El Adem – Lydda – Habbaniya – Bahrein – Mauripur – Poona, with 48-hour stops at Lydda and Mauripur. Further training, carrying freight, continued throughout April, and it was not long before the first passengers were to be carried. The first flight to India went as planned on 1 May. Some of the first arrivals on the first passenger return service a week later were liberated Prisoners of War from Rangoon. They were found to be fit to proceed, but suffering from the effects of malnutrition, exposure and lack of medical care while in Japanese hands.

VE Day, 8 May 1945, was celebrated at Merryfield. However, unlike at many other RAF airfields in the UK, the task of defeating the Japanese was still very much at the forefront of the minds of everyone at Merryfield, and their task continued. By the end of May the trooping flights to India were in full swing, with three aircraft leaving and three returning every two days. Each flight normally took 22 passengers.

For the next two and a half months scheduled services to the Far East were flown uneventfully from Merryfield. Supplies, equipment and passengers were flown out, and passengers – often liberated PoWs – were flown back. Then, on 14 August 1945, came the announcement of the Japanese surrender, and the celebration at Merryfield started. The following day, 15 August, marked the official surrender of the Japanese forces. On the same day 525 Squadron, based at Membury, began operating detachments of their Dakotas from Merryfield. They also contributed to the India services, bringing the schedule up to three departures and arrivals per day.

During the month of August incoming flights totalled 108 (2,075 passengers), and outgoing flights totalled 72 (1,515 passengers). Diversions during the month included Avro Yorks from Luqa to St Mawgan, and during the course of one day (29 August) twelve Halifaxes from Foggia, five Liberators from Castel Benito and a Lancaster from Iceland. All the passengers had to be fed and accommodated at Merryfield.

On 17 September 187 Squadron moved its trooping operation to Membury, with the main part of 525 Squadron. However, trooping was to continue from Merryfield following the arrival of 53

Liberators of 53 Squadron used Merryfield during 1945. (Aeroplane)

Squadron from St David's. A former Coastal Command squadron, 53 had been equipped with Liberators in its anti-submarine role since May 1943. In June 1945 it joined Transport Command, and with the installation of seats, oxygen equipment and portholes its Liberators were converted for trooping. At Merryfield the squadron started on the India run.

53 Squadron operated its services from Merryfield for the next two and a half months with few problems, but unfortunately, it did suffer one loss, the only fatal accident during the war years at Merryfield. Liberator KH126, captained by Flight Lieutenant Leopold Mielecki with a largely Polish crew, took off at 1000 hours on the morning of 22 November 1945. In the poor visibility the aircraft hit the hillside close to White's Farm, near Broadway Pound, caught fire and burnt out. Of the 22 passengers and six crew there was only one survivor found in the wreckage, the second pilot, Flying Officer Gordon Jenkins, but he died in the station sick quarters later that day. Soon after, on 3 December, 53 Squadron moved to Gransden Lodge and were to continue their transport services to India from the new base until the end of February 1946.

During November 1945 there were 32 flights into Merryfield (810 passengers) and 36 outgoing flights (913 passengers). The next arrival there was 242 Squadron, which arrived with Stirling transports from Stoney Cross on 9 December 1945. The squadron

Also flying from Merryfield in 1945 were the Yorks of 242 Squadron. (Aeroplane)

Sea Kings of the Fleet Air Arm were using Merryfield in 2006 for training. (Author)

had been a fighter squadron and had converted to the transport role just over a year earlier, flying services to the Far East from Stoney Cross. These it continued from Merryfield. The unit had some Avro Yorks while at Stoney Cross, but these were withdrawn. However, once the unit had settled down at Merryfield, Yorks reappeared on the squadron, and by January 1946 it was fully equipped with the new aircraft, which it flew to India, the Far East, and the Azores. 242 Squadron carried on with these services throughout the spring of 1946, but on 2 May it was moved to Oakington, where it was to continue its transport services.

With the departure of the Yorks of 242 Squadron Merryfield quickly ran down, there being no further demands for its facilities. The last aircraft to operate from the station at this time were the Oxfords of 152 (Radio Aids Training) Flight that had been detached to Merryfield for a few months and departed just before the station closed on 15 October 1946.

Merryfield was retained on a Care and Maintenance basis, and was reactivated in November 1951 for Flying Training Command. With the start of the Korean War and the perceived need for more

Royal Marines Lynx flies past Merryfield's refurbished wartime control tower.
(Author)

pilots, 208 Advanced Flying School was formed at the station on 19 November with Meteor and Vampire fighters. The threat passed, but the school continued at Merryfield until, as 9 FTS, as it had been retitled, it was disbanded in February 1955. Later in 1955 Merryfield was used for RAF Canberra deployments. Other users of the airfield during this period were the Westland Aircraft Co. – for flight testing of the Wyvern, and for air testing Sabres and Meteors rebuilt by them – and the Fleet Air Arm – for their shore-based operational Sea Venom squadrons.

The airfield was virtually abandoned from 1960, although it was still retained as government property on Care and Maintenance. Ten years later, the interest of the Royal Navy was once again aroused, and it was decided to reopen Merryfield as a satellite of Yeovilton. The control tower was refurbished and basic facilities constructed, including a small hangar. The airfield was named HMS *Heron II* and is still used for training by the commando helicopter squadrons of the Fleet Air Arm.

7

NORTH STOKE, GLOUCESTERSHIRE

3½ miles north-west of Bath
ST 717687

Because of the shortage of suitable landing fields for off-base flying training in 1943, Lansdowne racecourse was surveyed in May of that year as a potential site. Although the racecourse had not been used for several years, it was maintained in reasonable condition by its owners. Wing Commander Gosnell, Officer Commanding 3 Flying Instructors School (Advanced) (FIS(A)), travelled from Hullavington to inspect the racecourse, and found it to be acceptable as a Relief Landing Ground for his unit.

The course railings were removed, and after minimal preparation a runway was laid out on the grass in an east-west alignment and alternative landing and take-off runs were marked for secondary use. Soon the student pilots of 3 FIS(A) were to be seen flying their aircraft from the new landing ground, which was named North Stoke. These were mainly Airspeed Oxford twin-engined trainers, but the single-engined trainers also flown by the unit, such as the North American Harvard, Miles Magister, and Miles Master were occasionally to be seen at North Stoke. The school moved to Lulsgate Bottom in early October 1943, but continued to use North Stoke as its relief landing ground.

As indicated by the unit's title, the students of the school were in fact well-qualified pilots being trained as instructors. Because of its

Magisters were flown by 3 FIS(A) from North Stoke. (Author)

No 3 FIS(A) also operated Harvards. (Author)

location on the edge of a plateau with woods bordering two of its sides, North Stoke could be a tricky place to operate from at times and a challenging environment for the student instructors. Nonetheless there were few incidents; the only serious one recorded involved an Oxford, which was badly damaged during a landing on 7 March 1945.

3 FIS(A) was disbanded on 5 July 1945, but its aircraft and staff were absorbed by 7 FIS(A), also at Lulsgate. This unit continued to use North Stoke for training. However this was not to be for long as, with the war in Europe already over by then, the need for pilots started to diminish. By mid-August the end of the war in the East was in sight, with the Japanese showing signs that they wanted to surrender. Having no further need for it, the RAF therefore handed North Stoke airfield back to its owners on 22 August 1945. Bath (Lansdowne) racecourse was reinstated over the ensuing months, and soon became part of the post-war racing scene. The site's connection with aviation remains, however, as it has a helipad for use during race meetings.

8
WATCHET
(DONIFORD)

1 mile east of Watchet
ST 092432

A small grass airstrip was established in 1928 near the town of Watchet, on the Somerset coast. This was to provide communications for the camp that had been established there alongside the gunnery range in Bridgwater Bay. Various army units would attend the camp during the summer for anti-aircraft gunnery training. Targets were provided by the RAF, flying from an airfield at Weston Zoyland, 19 miles roughly to the east. Hawker Horsleys were used to tow target drogues on long (!) wires for the army gunners to shoot at.

Trials with unmanned target aircraft took place at Watchet during the summer of 1937. The aircraft used was a DH Queen Bee, a derivative of the Tiger Moth built specifically as a live-gunnery flying target. In contrast to the Tiger Moth's metal-frame, fabric-covered fuselage, the Queen Bee had a wooden ply-covered one for cheapness and buoyancy. It was usually flown as a twin-float seaplane, to enable its recovery should it be shot down over the gunnery ranges, the majority of which were over the sea. The intention was that the aircraft should be recovered after a target practice flight and then flown again after the registration of any hits and the repair of any damage. Any total losses were put down to

DH Queen Bee floatplane on the catapult ready for launch. (Aeroplane)

bad luck, as this meant fewer targets for anyone else! A total of 380 Queen Bees were built between 1935 and 1944.

Because of its float undercarriage, the Queen Bee had to be launched from a catapult. As one wasn't available at Watchet, the first flight of a Queen Bee over the range was made by courtesy of the Royal Navy, the cruiser *HMS Neptune* launching K5100 on 29 July 1935. The aircraft was successfully landed near the cruiser later in the day and hoisted aboard for more trial flights. Later a catapult was built on the cliffs in the gun park at Doniford and the first successful launch was made on 3 August 1937 by No.1 Anti-Aircraft Co-operation Unit, based at RAF Henlow.

On 11 April 1939, Z Flight of 1 Anti-Aircraft Co-operation Unit was formed at Watchet with eight Queen Bees. It also flew Avro

Tutors and Miles Magisters on communications duties. The unit's headquarters were at RAF Biggin Hill. Queen Bees were flown successfully during that summer's firing camp; several aircraft were hit, but only one was shot down, and one crashed into the sea. The surviving aircraft were taken to Henlow for storage for the winter.

The following spring, Z Flight returned to Watchet from its winter quarters and resumed flying its Queen Bees for the anti-aircraft gunnery camps. Some of these aircraft had been ferried to Watchet from Henlow by AACU pilots and were then fitted with floats in order to be launched from the catapult. Drogue targets were also used, towed by the Hawker Henleys flown by A Flight of 1 AACU, based at Weston Zoyland. Following the outbreak of war in September 1939, Z Flight was joined by X Flight from Henlow as the gunnery training at Watchet took on a specific purpose.

Training continued into the winter of 1939 without a break and intensified with the large number of army units then coming through. Although many Queen Bees were hit, few were lost. An exception to the general rule was P4684, which, on the afternoon of

Lysander of 16 Squadron, one of the regular users of Watchet. (Aeroplane)

Also seen at Watchet from 1943 onwards were the Piper L-4 Cubs of the USAAF. (Author)

22 July 1940, flew for 50 minutes after it had been launched from the catapult. It was then engaged and was hit by the fifth shell of a salvo of seven. The aircraft went out of control, dived vertically into the sea, and was totally destroyed. This was the last Queen Bee to be lost at Watchet, for shortly afterwards both X and Z Flight were transferred to other ranges, in Wales. Target facilities were then provided by the Henleys of A Flight, based at Weston Zoyland.

The airstrip at Watchet remained in use for communications and training. It was often used by the Lysanders of No 16 Squadron, based at Weston Zoyland, for practice short-field landings during 1941, and the early part of 1942 until the squadron re-equipped with Mustangs. The airstrip was also a useful emergency landing ground for single-engined aircraft, such as the Henleys of 1 AACU, if they developed engine problems. However, as the tug aircraft became larger and more powerful, the field became of limited

The site of the airstrip at Watchet can still be identified today. (Author)

value in this role. Nevertheless, communications aircraft continued to use Watchet, Austers becoming frequent visitors in 1942 and 1943. Their US equivalent, the Piper L-4 Cub, also put in appearances at Watchet when US Army units began to use the range. This level of activity continued into 1944 as the build-up to the invasion of France took place, but reduced during the autumn of 1944 and the summer of 1945.

After the war closure of the air strip seemed imminent, but in July 1947 Watchet became the Light Anti-Aircraft Gunnery School of the RAF Regiment. Other RAF Regiment units used the range until 1956, but, with the availability of alternative facilities, Watchet was closed in February 1957. Little remains today to indicate its past role.

9
WESTON-SUPER-MARE

1½ miles south-east of Weston-super-Mare
ST 344603

The decision by Weston-super-Mare UDC to open an airfield in the
1930s could well have been influenced by the efforts of Sir Alan
Cobham. He promoted aviation in Britain during the inter-war
years and in 1929 toured the country in an attempt to persuade
local authorities to build their own airfields. Over a six-month
period he initiated his 'Municipal Aerodromes Scheme' and visited
over one hundred towns and cities in his de Havilland DH61 eight-
seater, single-engined biplane *Youth of Britain*.

Work began on the construction of Weston Airport in February
1936, and by May scheduled passenger flights were started by
Railway Air Services. They flew DH84 Dragon twin-engined
biplanes on a new service that went from Plymouth to Haldon, to
Cardiff, and on to Weston before going to Bristol (Whitchurch). A
main passenger terminal and administration building was
completed in 1938, along with a large side-opening hangar, and in
October of that year Western Airways started flying the first
scheduled night services in Britain, using DH89 Dragon Rapides
from Weston.

Also in 1938 the Royal Air Force opened a school of technical
training at Locking, a mile or so east of Weston Airport. Although
the school was unusual for an RAF establishment in that it was not
located at an airfield, this was not seen as a handicap because of the
convenience of the nearby airport. In due course Locking Station
Flight was set up at Weston to provide communications and

Weston-super-Mare airport seen in the summer of 1939. (Aeroplane)

training facilities for the school. The RAF presence at Weston increased the following year when the Air Ministry placed a contract that resulted in the formation of 39 Elementary and Reserve Flying Training School at the airport. It was one of several such schools that had been set up following a decision in 1935 by the director of training that elementary flying training would be carried out by civilian flying schools, leaving the RAF's flying training schools to concentrate on more advanced training. This in turn relieved front-line squadrons of training their newly-posted in pilots under what was later termed 'operational conversion'. As their title implied the E&RFTSs were also responsible for the training of reservists. 39 E&RFTS was operated by the Straight Corporation, which also owned Weston Airways. The school opened on 3 July 1939, training its students on Miles Magisters, and Hawker Audax and Hind trainers.

With the prospect of war, the flying training system was reviewed and the roles of aircrew in relation to the new and more

Magister trainers were flown from Weston by No 39 E&RFTS. (Author)

No 39 E&RFTS also flew Hind trainers. (Aeroplane)

complex aircraft then coming into service were looked at. For example, the job of Observer was expanded to include navigation, bomb aiming and gunnery. To put this new training system into effect some schools were closed, some re-roled, and others expanded, the aim being to increase the number of trained personnel being produced. At Weston-super-Mare this resulted on 2 September 1939, the eve of the declaration of war, in the closure of 39 E&RFTS, its aircraft being transferred to other flying schools. In its place a new school was formed under contract to the Straight Corporation. This was No 5 Civil Air Navigation School, which was formed on the day that 39 E&RFTS was closed and utilized its facilities and many of its staff. 5 CANS was to take on the role of providing navigation training to RAF Observers and Navigators formerly given by the E&RFTSs as part of pilot training. Equipped with Avro Anson twin-engined trainers, the unit was quickly at work. However, things were soon to change. On 1 November 1939, 5 CANS became 5 Air Observer and Navigation School and was taken under RAF control. The unit continued to train Observers and Navigators, using airspace to the west of its base, over the Bristol Channel, Wales and the Irish Sea, away from likely enemy air activity. On 12 June the school absorbed 3 AONS, which was transferred from Desford in Leicestershire.

However, 5 AONS itself was not to remain an entity for too much longer. By the late summer of 1940 pilot training in various parts of the British Empire was well established under the Empire Air Training Scheme. Apart from being well away from hostile enemy action, the much better weather meant that the duration of flying training courses could more or less be guaranteed. The scheme was so successful that it was decided to include Navigator training, and 5 AONS was one of the first such units to be involved. On 22 August 1940 the school closed at Weston-super-Mare and packed its equipment for transfer to South Africa, reopening at Oudtshoorn airfield on 4 November 1940. A week later, under further reorganization, it became 45 Air School of the South African Air Force.

On the outbreak of war, all civil flying in Britain was stopped from 3 September 1939, apart from a limited number of authorized flights. This included some passenger services, and in late October Weston Airways restarted a limited service to Cardiff. However,

Ansons were flown by No 5 CANS (later 5 AONS). (Aeroplane)

this did not last for long, probably due to a lack of passengers. The company's maintenance facilities were then occupied dealing with locally-based and visiting aircraft belonging to the RAF, which took over the airfield on 1 May 1940. Waterlogging had been a problem at Weston-super-Mare, and so around this time a main runway of 4,197 feet was laid on a south-west/north-east axis. There were two other runways, of 2,950 and 2,260 feet, laid out on the grass.

During the summer of 1940, while training carried on from Weston-super-Mare, a shadow factory was being built by the Ministry of Aircraft Production at Old Mixon, to the west of the airfield. The purpose of the factory was to build the Bristol Beaufighter, an important new type that had been ordered into quantity production, the main Bristol factory being unable to build enough to meet the RAF's requirements. Old Mixon was also a useful back-up facility should the main factory be attacked. The factory was completed in the autumn and production of the Beaufighter started in September. For a period output of Beaufighters was restricted because of a shortage of components.

Beaufighters in production at Bristol's Old Mixon factory. (Aeroplane)

These were produced mainly in Coventry, which was hit hard by the Luftwaffe during the period in 1940 known as the Blitz. However, many of the manufacturers managed to restore their facilities and were soon supplying Old Mixon.

Following the departure of 5 AONS, it was not long before their place at Weston was taken by another training unit. This was 10 EFTS, which arrived on 7 September 1940. The school had been operating from Yatesbury in Wiltshire but was moved out because of the expansion of 2 Radio School, that was also based there. Yatesbury was a much larger airfield than Weston, and so 10 EFTS flying training methods had to be changed to suit the smaller airfield. Lulsgate soon became available for circuits and general flying training, which eased things at Weston-super-Mare. There was, however, a shortage of technical and hangar accommodation at the latter, and on 12 November a fierce gale that wrecked two huts also damaged eleven of the school's 30 Tiger Moths that were picketed to the ground.

In order to protect Weston-super-Mare from air attack, a Q-decoy site was built two miles to the south, at Bleadon. In fact the

Luftwaffe paid little attention to Weston, but on at least two occasions when they did appear the Q-site proved invaluable. The first of these was in January 1941 when a heavy raid was mounted on the town of Weston-super-Mare. Before the German bombers could find the airfield the Q-site was lit, and they immediately turned their attention in that direction. The site was heavily cratered, but its effectiveness that night was mainly due to AC2 Bright, who was part of the crew manning the site. When the remote-controlled igniters failed to operate, he left the safety of the control bunker and lit the decoy fire devices by hand, a feat for which he was later decorated. The site was bombed again in May, when over a dozen high explosive bombs were dropped on the simulated runway flarepath, and no damage resulted from the raid in the town or on the airfield.

10 EFTS carried on with its training task into 1941, but in June of that year Lulsgate was closed to training, and this resulted once again in more congestion at Weston-super-Mare. The school put up with these conditions for a few more months, but in September it was moved to the more spacious Stoke Orchard airfield. With the departure of 10 EFTS, Weston-super-Mare turned from being a very busy airfield to a fairly quiet one. The Locking Station Flight remained and it accounted for most of the flying over the next twelve months or so, in addition to the test flying and ferrying of Beaufighters from the Old Mixon factory.

In 10 October 1942, 286 Squadron arrived from Colerne with their Hurricanes, Defiants and Oxfords. They flew target facilities sorties for anti-aircraft units throughout the South West, and used Weston-super-Mare as an HQ, from which numerous detachments were made throughout the rest of Somerset, as well as Cornwall, Devon and Dorset. In April 1943, Weston-super-Mare was transferred to Technical Training Command under the control of RAF Locking. The Equipment Training School was established at the airport in August, having been moved in from Eastbourne.

286 Squadron continued to use the airfield as its base through the autumn and into the winter of 1943, but on 29 November it moved again, this time to Weston Zoyland, across the Somerset levels to the south-west. It was replaced by a detachment of 116 Squadron, based at Croydon. The detachment's role was to test the calibration of anti-aircraft gun radar systems at units throughout the South

Tempests were flown by the ATDU from Weston. This example is now part of the RAF Museum. (Author)

West and South Wales. The main part of their work involved flying over a designated area within the radar's search cone, at a pre-determined speed and height. This called for accurate flying, but some pilots considered the task mundane. Nonetheless, up to a dozen Oxfords were based at Weston-super-Mare at any one time to undertake this task, and the detachment's crews were kept busy, as their services were in great demand. Like 286 Squadron, the squadron provided a vital and important function in keeping Britain's anti-aircraft defences well prepared.

In March 1944, a detachment of the Aircraft Torpedo Development Unit (ATDU) transferred to Weston-super-Mare from Weston Zoyland. As its name implied, the ATDU role was to develop the application of new air-dropped torpedos and methods for their use. Using weapons ranges in the Bristol Channel for its trials, the unit employed a variety of aircraft types, including Swordfish, Beaufighters, and later Mosquitos and Tempests, to drop the torpedoes and also to act as chase planes to monitor and

Proctors were used by the Weston Station Flight. (Author)

photograph the drops. The detachment was to remain at Weston-super-Mare until 1949.

Beaufighter production was building up well at Old Mixon during 1943, and by early 1944 it reached its peak at 87 aeroplanes completed per month. The Beaufighter was a versatile aircraft that was able to perform most defensive and offensive roles effectively, with little or no modification required. A wide range of marks was built at Old Mixon, from the Mark IF fighter, through the Mark IV fighter and torpedo bomber, to the Marks X and XI anti-shipping and strike aircraft. Production of the Beaufighter finished in September 1945 when the last aircraft, SR919, a Mark X, rolled off the line at Old Mixon. Altogether, of the 5,564 Beaufighters built in the UK (a further 364 were built under licence in Australia), 3,096 were constructed at Old Mixon. The Beaufighter turned out to be one of the most enduring types of the Second World War, continuing in service with the RAF as a target tug until May 1960, over 20 years after its maiden flight.

The end of the war had meant no major changes in military flying from Weston-super-Mare, as the ATDU continued to operate, along with the RAF Locking Station Flight then flying Percival

Proctors. Civil flying was, however, resumed, initially with scheduled services to Cardiff. Custody of the airfield was therefore transferred to the Ministry of Civil Aviation.

With the end of Beaufighter production at the Bristol Aeroplane factory, the manufacture of components, including those for helicopters, was resumed. In March 1955 it was decided to centralize all rotary-wing work at Old Mixon, and the Bristol Aircraft Helicopter Division was moved there from Filton, together with production of the Bristol Sycamore helicopter. This type was succeeded in production by the Belvedere twin-rotor tactical transport helicopter for the RAF. The Belvedere was still under development in February 1960 when the Bristol Helicopter Division was taken over by Westland Helicopters Ltd. The manufacture of helicopter components was then to continue at the site until 2002. Civil and military flying carried on from Weston-super-Mare until the mid-1990s. Nowadays the only flying at the airfield is from the Helicopter Museum, which was established in 1989 with a few helicopters. It now houses more than 70, on a 4½ acre site that includes some of the original 1936 airport buildings.

10
WESTON ZOYLAND

4 miles south-east of Bridgwater
ST 365344

Situated on the Somerset Levels, an area of low-lying drained
marshland in the centre of the county, Weston Zoyland airfield is in
a flat area just east of Weston Zoyland village, between the main
road to Bridgwater and the King's Sedgemoor Drain. It was first
used as a landing field by target tug aircraft flying on the gunnery
ranges off Watchet, in Bridgwater Bay. This activity started in 1926,
and the airfield was used for this purpose every summer. Buildings
were gradually added and the landing ground enlarged, so that by
1939 Weston Zoyland was a well-established airfield.

With the outbreak of war in September 1939, the seasonal nature
of activity at Watchet changed and training continued into the
winter. The target tug aircraft of A Flight, No. 1 Anti-Aircraft Unit
were permanently based at Weston Zoyland, having been detached
from the unit's HQ at Biggin Hill. The Westland Wallaces that the
unit had flown during earlier camps had been replaced by Hawker
Henley purpose-built target tugs, which were supplemented by
Fairey Battles and Westland Lysanders, and later by Boulton Paul
Defiants.

A detachment of 16 Squadron flew its Lysanders to Weston
Zoyland in November 1939 for a spell of army co-operation
training before rejoining the main squadron at its base at Old

Sarum in Wiltshire. The unit was earmarked to join the air component of the British Expeditionary Force, but did not leave for France and its base at Bertangles until April 1940. With the onset of the German offensive a few weeks later, the squadron's Lysanders were involved in tactical reconnaissance for Allied units in the Le Cateau and St Quentin areas. Several aircraft were lost by 16 Squadron in the subsequent fighting, but it claimed two enemy aircraft in return. Back in the UK, the squadron was initially based at Lympne; it then moved around several other airfields before returning to Weston Zoyland on 14 August 1940. It was to remain at the station for the greater part of the ensuing two and a half years.

Soon after their return to Somerset, 16 Squadron's Lysanders were once again engaged on operations, flying dawn and dusk coastal reconnaissance patrols in search of potential enemy invasion forces. The patrols continued through the winter and covered the coastline of Somerset, Devon and Cornwall. The

Lysanders of 16 Squadron, which were regular visitors and residents at the airfield from 1939 to 1942. (Aeroplane)

Tiger Moths were operated from Weston Zoyland by 8 AACU. (Aeroplane)

squadron also mounted air-sea rescue patrols until later in the summer, when it reverted to army co-operation training with ground units. A new Lysander squadron, No. 239, came into existence within Army Co-operation Command on 18 September 1940. To enable this to take place, 16 Squadron transferred one of its flights to Hatfield, where the new squadron was formed.

16 Squadron was soon joined by 8 AACU, which was transferred from Filton. Flying a variety of aircraft, including Tiger Moths and Oxfords, the unit was tasked to provide training for anti-aircraft units in the Bristol and north Somerset area. RAF Weston Zoyland became a self-accounting station on 1 September 1940, in recognition of its stand-alone status and role. However, the increase in personnel based at the station put pressure on its limited accommodation, and airmen had to be billeted on householders in the nearby villages of Middlezoy and Othery, as well as in Weston Zoyland itself.

In December 1940 a detachment of the Special Duty Flight arrived at Weston Zoyland. Based at Christchurch in Dorset, this was a trials unit attached to the Air Ministry Research Establishment in Swanage in Dorset. Its work included the research and development of radio, telecommunications, and radar equipment. With two Lysanders and a de Havilland Fox Moth, the detachment spent the best part of a year at Weston Zoyland, undertaking radar airborne interception trials with a team from the Air Defence Experimental Establishment, based at Christchurch.

Weston Zoyland is only 30 feet above sea level and the surrounding area is often very damp, which makes it prone to fog. However, its unusual weather patterns meant that it was often open when other airfields in the West Country were not. Early in 1941 a number of aircraft being ferried across the Bay of Biscay to Gibraltar had to return to the UK because of bad weather. They were diverted to Weston Zoyland, as the only airfield that was open in the area at the time. This event seemed to prove the value of Weston Zoyland, and a series of developments followed, the first being to improve accommodation.

During the summer of 1941 both units based at Weston Zoyland were busy with their commitments, and in June two tragic events befell 16 Squadron. On the 9th, the newly appointed CO, Wing Commander Hancock, was killed when the squadron's Percival Proctor communications aircraft P6256 crashed on take-off from Roborough near Plymouth. Two days later his appointed replacement, Squadron Leader Walker, was flying his Lysander III V9510 near Exmouth on the Devon coast, when the aircraft was attacked by four Messerschmitt Bf109s. Although the Lysander's gunner managed to shoot down one of the attackers, the British aircraft was soon overwhelmed and destroyed by the remaining fighters, killing both crew.

The Lysanders of 239 Squadron, that had been formed with the assistance of 16 Squadron the previous September, arrived at Weston Zoyland on 6 May 1941, from their base at Gatwick. They had been detached as the first unit to use Weston Zoyland in its new role as the major practice camp for the RAF Army co-operation squadrons. As well as the Watchet range, the squadrons in training were able to use ranges at Steart Flats and Lilstock for bombing and other armament practice. To add to the target-towing facilities available at Weston Zoyland, P Flight of 1 AACU was formed there on 25 August 1941, with Henleys, Lysanders and Defiants. A

Henleys were flown by No 1 AACU from Weston Zoyland. (Aeroplane)

further target facilities unit, 1492 (Target Towing) Flight, was formed at the station on 18 October, equipped initially with the Lysander, which was later supplemented with and then replaced by the Master, Martinet and Mosquito. 241 Squadron, with Lysanders, flew in from Bottisham on 8 October for a short stay, and it was followed by 140 Squadron on 29 October. This was a PR unit based at Benson, with Spitfires and Blenheims. The last unit to use the station for the year's practice camp was 268 Squadron, a Lysander unit based at Snailwell, which arrived on 25 November and stayed until mid-December 1941.

On 7 February 1942, a new type appeared at Weston Zoyland that was to become a familiar sight there: the North American

Mustang single-seat fighter, flown in by the pilots of 26 Squadron. They had been detached from their base at Gatwick for an armament practice camp. The squadron was also equipped with the Curtiss Tomahawk, which flew alongside the unit's Mustangs until it was replaced almost a year later. 16 Squadron started to re-equip with the Mustang I in April 1942. Although manufactured in the USA, the aircraft had been designed to meet a British specification.

Other US manufacturers were busy on their own projects in 1940 when North American offered to build the aircraft for the RAF. Although the company had never built a fighter before, they were given the job by the Air Ministry Buying Mission, which had been established in the USA shortly before. The result was an aeroplane that was a superb performer at low altitudes, but its effectiveness fell off dramatically at higher altitudes. Subsequently, its

Mustang of 26 Squadron which was the first unit with the type to use Weston Zoyland, in February 1942. (Aeroplane)

147

performance was greatly improved by the installation of the Rolls-Royce Merlin in place of the original US Allison engine. The aircraft was also adopted by the USAAF, and in its later form became one of the outstanding aircraft of the Second World War. However, the Mustang was initially issued in its original form to RAF squadrons for tactical reconnaissance and ground attack. Most of the squadrons that received Mustangs had previously flown Lysanders, and the contrast between the two aircraft was huge. The arrival of the Mustang also meant a change of tactics, for the Mustang could not land in farmers' fields or loiter at low speed. The squadrons' role therefore had to change to reflect the higher speeds and better firepower of their new mount. For 16 Squadron this meant type conversion, tactical training, and operational evaluation in order to get the best out of the Mustang.

1942 was to be the year of the Mustang for Weston Zoyland. As well as the visit by 26 Squadron, followed by 16 Squadron's conversion to the type, several other Mustang units were to appear at the station. The first of these, on 15 June, was 170 Squadron, which formed at Weston Zoyland on Mustang Is in the fighter reconnaissance role. It did not stay at the station for long, and within the week had moved to its new base at Hurn. 171 Squadron was the next to arrive at Weston Zoyland when it flew in for its armament camp on 10 September. Like 26 Squadron it too had Tomahawks and Mustangs, although the former were to be replaced by the end of the year. After its ten-day camp the unit returned to its base at Gatwick. Other squadrons to visit Weston Zoyland for training during the rest of the year were, on 13 October, 169 Squadron with Mustang Is, from Doncaster, and 63 Squadron from Gatwick, whose Mustangs flew in on 6 November.

In the meantime, by October 1942, 16 Squadron had been cleared for operations, and mounted its first mission with the Mustang, a convoy patrol in the Channel, on the 10th. Further operations followed, code-named 'Lagoons', which were patrols and sweeps across the Channel and along the French coast looking for targets of opportunity. These provided valuable operational experience and resulted in a number of targets being destroyed, but they were not without risk: the squadron lost two aircraft on these operations in November, and another in December. Towards the end of the month the squadron received orders to move, and on 2 January

148

1943 the Mustangs of 16 Squadron left Weston Zoyland for their new base at Andover in Hampshire.

There were other changes at Weston Zoyland during the winter of 1942–43. On 1 November A Flight and P Flight of 1 AACU were disbanded and re-formed as anti-aircraft co-operation flights: A Flight became 1600 (Anti-Aircraft Co-operation) Flight and P Flight became 1601 (Anti-Aircraft Co-operation) Flight. Both units continued with their task of providing drogue targets for anti-aircraft gunners to fire at and of making simulated attacks on gun positions to assist the gunners in identifying and tracking potential targets. For the job they had a mix of aircraft, including Henley TT III, Martinet TT I and Defiant TT I target tugs, along with Fairey Battle T and de Havilland Tiger Moth trainers.

A new, but similar, unit also came into being on 20 January 1943, under the unwieldy title of No. 1 RAF Regiment Anti-Aircraft Practice Camp Target Towing Flight. Flying Lysanders, the flight fulfilled its title by providing targets purely for RAF Regiment detachments, mainly at Watchet. The unit was disbanded a few months later, on 17 June, and re-formed as No. 1625 (Anti-Aircraft Co-operation) Flight, with Martinets added to its complement.

Martinets were flown by several units from Weston Zoyland. (Aeroplane)

Weston Zoyland had become an important station by late 1942, but because of its low-lying position it suffered from water-logging. It was therefore decided to upgrade the airfield to bomber standard by providing long, wide runways and taxiways, along with other facilities. Additional land had to be requisitioned to enable runways of sufficient length to be laid out, and this included the closure of the main A372 road and its re-routing to the south. Construction work began in the spring of 1943. Three runways were laid, the main one, of 5,775 feet, running roughly east–west, a secondary one of 4,101 feet running roughly north-west/south-east, and a third, of 3,564 feet, in a north-east/south-west direction. Four large hangars were constructed, two (both T2s) on the southern side of the airfield and two (one T2 and one Bellman) on the northern side. A Bessoneau cawas hangar and nine blister hangars were also erected around the airfield. Two large pan-handle hardstands were laid on the western side of the site, and 33 loop dispersals were provided, leading off the perimeter track around the airfield's boundary. A large two-storey watch office (or control tower) was built, along with all the necessary ancillary operational and technical buildings that were not already provided. The living site situated to the north-west was upgraded and enlarged, so that it could accommodate 1,530 personnel.

During the reconstruction period, the station remained open and flying operations continued as far as possible. The resident squadrons flew their target facilities missions, and visiting units arrived for armament practice camps and other training.

On 1 June 1943 Army Co-operation Command was disbanded and reorganized as the Second Tactical Air Force, in preparation for the Allied invasion of Europe. The new formation was to bring together all the tactical squadrons of the RAF, including bombers, fighter bombers, fighter escorts, and tactical reconnaissance and support squadrons, so that they could train together in preparation for the invasion. This brought a new sense of purpose to the training at Weston Zoyland. More Mustang I squadrons arrived for their armament training in July, including 231 Squadron from Dunsfold and 414 Squadron from Gatwick, which stayed until mid-August.

Following completion of the new runways, it was decided to create a transport squadron, 525 Squadron, which was formed at

Warwick CIII transport, of 525 Squadron at Weston Zoyland in late 1943. (Aeroplane)

Weston Zoyland on 2 September. Its initial equipment was the Vickers Warwick I twin-engined transport, a development of the Wellington bomber. The squadron immediately started training and working up to operational standard. By November it was cleared for operations and began flying a scheduled passenger service from Weston Zoyland to Gibraltar.

Spitfire squadrons had started to use Weston Zoyland in the autumn of 1943. They included 19 Squadron, which flew its Spitfire IXs down from Kingsnorth in late September, and 122 Squadron, also with the Spitfire IX, which arrived for its armament practice camp in mid-October. 1492 (TT) Flight disbanded at Weston Zoyland on 18 October 1943, but was immediately re-formed with Masters, Martinets and Hurricanes as 13 Armament Practice Camp. 286 Squadron arrived at Weston Zoyland on 29 November, on transfer from RAF Locking. The new arrivals were from the HQ element of the squadron, which was another target facilities unit. The role of 286 Squadron was, like many other units that had passed through Weston Zoyland, to provide target facilities, but in

Vultee Vengeances were operated by 587 Squadron from Weston Zoyland. (Aeroplane)

this case for units of all three services right across the South West. As with similar units, targets for the guns were towed by target tugs such as the Martinet or Defiant, or aircraft such as the Oxford, Master and Hurricane, over anti-aircraft units at predetermined heights and speeds for tracking practice, or to calibrate the gunnery equipment. Detachments of the squadron were taken all over the South West to fly for the guns, and based themselves at convenient RAF stations for the duration of their deployment.

Two days after 286 Squadron's arrival at Weston Zoyland, another unit came into being in the form of 587 Squadron, which resulted from the amalgamation of 1600, 1601 and 1625 (AA Co-op) Flights. Its initial equipment, inherited from the flights, consisted of Henleys, Martinets, Oxfords and Hurricanes. The unit was formed to supplement the work of 286 Squadron, providing anti-aircraft co-operation duties for anti-aircraft units across the South West, and in South Wales. The last visitors of 1943 were the Auster Mk IIIs of 653 Squadron, an army co-operation squadron based at Penshurst. These aircraft represented the other side of the coin from the Mustangs, undertaking a role more akin to that of the Lysanders than to the high-speed tactical reconnaissance of the fighter aircraft.

The work of the Weston Zoyland squadrons continued into 1944, their efforts being in great demand. During January, both 286 and 587 Squadrons found the time to undertake trials on a new concept, which was that of using towing-target gliders, rather than drogues. Although the trials were successful, the concept was never taken up in general service.

In February 1944 525 Squadron moved to RAF Lyneham, to continue its scheduled services from there, and within a few months there were to be other departures from Weston Zoyland. In the build-up to the invasion, the US Ninth Air Force needed to move one of its troop carrier wings, namely the 50th Troop Carrier Wing of IX Troop Carrier Command, nearer to the Channel coast. The Americans requested the use of several airfields in the South West of England, and were offered four by the RAF: Exeter, Merryfield, Upottery and Weston Zoyland. This meant that the resident RAF units had to relocate, and so 13 Armament Practice Camp moved out, followed on 10 April 1944 by 286 and 587 Squadrons, which transferred to Culmhead. Also included in the move – in this case, along the Somerset coast to Weston-super-Mare – was a detachment of the Aircraft Torpedo Development Unit that had come to Weston Zoyland to mount torpedo trials in the Bristol Channel, flying a variety of aeroplanes, including Swordfish and Beaufighters. Most of the RAF ground support staff also departed, leaving a small cadre of personnel to keep the essential services going until the USAAF took over.

The group allocated to Weston Zoyland was the 442nd Troop Carrier Group, which flew, like most of the squadrons of the IX Troop Carrier Command, the Douglas C-47 Skytrain (known to the British as the Dakota). By the early summer of 1944 the group had 96 C-47s on strength. Although advance parties of the USAAF personnel had arrived at Weston Zoyland during May, the move was delayed because of D-Day, then scheduled to start on the night of 4th June. Operations for D-Day (which was delayed by 24 hours) were therefore mounted from their base in Fulbeck, Lincolnshire. The group sent 45 C-47s, carrying paratroops of the Second Airborne Division, to drop zones near St Mère Église in Normandy.

Three C-47s were lost during the operation and 31 were damaged. The group flew a re-supply mission to the beachhead on the following day, without loss. Shortly after this the group started its move to Weston Zoyland. One by one, the four squadrons of the 442nd Troop Carrier Group (the 303rd, 304th, 305th and 306th) moved to Weston Zoyland and by mid-June they were settled in at their new base. In the meantime, US Army engineers had arrived at the airfield to lay pierced-steel planking, in order to assist the manœuvering of gliders and their tugs for airborne operations. Some 800 feet were laid by the engineers on either side of each end of the main runway.

For the next few months the local area resounded to the sound of Pratt and Witney twin Wasp engines as the C-47s of the 442nd TCG flew repeated training sorties. As well as C-47s, the group had a similar number of Waco GC-4A gliders (also known as the Hadrian) on strength. The glider pilots were, like the C-47 pilots, also members of the group's personnel (as opposed to British glider pilots, who were members of the British Army's Glider Pilot Regiment, as distinct from the RAF squadrons that towed them into action). In addition to training, the C-47s were used on transport duties, taking freight and equipment to the Continent and often returning with casualties for treatment in the UK or for repatriation to the USA. In mid-July, three of the squadrons were deployed to Follonica in Italy. From there they participated in Operation Dragoon, the Allied landings in southern France, that took place in August. The 306th TCS had remained at Weston Zoyland and, during the absence of the other squadrons, maintained the airfreight services to the Continent.

The group took part in the next major airborne operation of the war, Operation Market Garden, which was a bold initiative to project an Allied armoured thrust across the Rhine into Germany. British and US paratroops were to be dropped to capture bridges en route, so that the ground forces could reach the last bridge at Arnhem. The 442nd TCG were briefed to lift paratroops of the 101st Airborne Division that were to capture the canal crossings between Eindhoven and Veghel along the first part of the route. With the approach of Operation Market, the airborne phase of the operation, however, it was decided to move the group to an advance base at Chilbolton in Hampshire, which was nearer to the target area.

At 1311 hours on 17 September 1944, the first of 90 C-47s of the 442nd TCG took off from Chilbolton. They formed up and headed for the wing assembly point over Hatfield. There they joined a column of 424 aircraft taking 6,695 paratroops of the 101st Airborne Division to their drop zones near Son and Veghel in Holland. They met fierce anti-aircraft fire near the DZs, but, although three of the group's C-47s were shot down, the majority of the paratroops were successfully dropped onto their DZs.

The following day, 80 C-47s took off, towing gliders carrying reinforcements, jeeps and equipment. Although one of the group's gliders was forced to ditch, its occupants being swiftly rescued by the vigilant Allied air-sea rescue patrols, the remainder reached their LZs. However, bad weather ensured that on 19 September, of the 81 gliders that left Chilbolton towed behind the group's C-47s, only 28 reached the LZs. Seven gliders went down into the sea, along with two C-47s. The remaining gliders had to put down away from the LZs, but some, as well as two of the C-47s, were shot down. A reduced effort on 20 September was a final drop to the 101st Airborne. This involved the 442nd TCG, which flew 20 C-47s from Greenham Common, dropping supplies, and twelve more, from Ramsbury, which dropped reinforcements. During Operation Market, the 442nd TCG lost ten aircraft, one of the highest losses among the 14 US C-47 groups that took part. It then returned to Weston Zoyland and resumed transport operations, taking supplies and equipment to France and the Low Countries. Towards the end of September the group was given notice of a move to the Continent, and on 4 October it started moving out. Within two days the last of the C-47s had departed. This was the last of the 50th TCW groups to leave its base in Britain.

Having been notified of the USAAF move, the RAF was quick to return its units to Weston Zoyland. 286 Squadron was the first to appear, on transfer from Zeals, arriving at Weston Zoyland on 28 September as the Americans were preparing to move out. They were followed by 587 Squadron from Culmhead. Both squadrons immediately resumed their tasks from the station, as their services were still in demand. At that time they were both flying the Martinet TT I target tug, the Oxford I and II and the Hurricane IIC and IV. Shortly after their return to Weston Zoyland, 286 Squadron received the Miles Master III, and 587 Squadron the Vultee

Vengeance III, a US dive-bomber modified for target-towing work. The two target facilities squadrons remained the sole occupants of Weston Zoyland until February 1945, when 1540 (Blind Approach Training) Flight moved in with its Oxfords from Lulsgate Bottom. The flight provided instrument flying facilities for the pupils of 6 (P) Advanced Flying Unit at Little Rissington.

Although VE Day, 8 May 1945,was celebrated in style at Weston Zoyland, the end of the war in Europe brought changes to the station. A general run down of activities began, starting with the disbandment of 286 Squadron on 16 May. Another target facilities squadron, No. 285, arrived at Weston Zoyland from North Weald on 20 June, only to disband six days later. With the reorganization of training units, 1540 (BAT) Flight ceased to work with 6 (P)AFU in July and instead started working with 3 (P)AFU, based at South Cerney. The flight continued to fly from Weston Zoyland until it disbanded on 17 December. Meanwhile other units passed through

Aerial view of Weston Zoyland, seen from a microlight in July 2005. (Neil Holt)

the station. On 5 September the Tempest Mk Vs of 222 Squadron arrived at Weston Zoyland, on return from Airfield B155 (Dedelstorf) in Holland. They stayed for several weeks before moving on to Molesworth on 23 October.

Although activity at Weston Zoyland generally reduced during the early part of 1946, the nearby ranges remained open, and in April another target facilities unit, 691 Squadron, arrived from Exeter. It flew Vengeance and Martinet target tugs, along with Harvards and Spitfire XVIs. It supplemented and then replaced 587 Squadron, which moved to Tangmere on 1 June 1946. In turn, 691 Squadron was not to remain at Weston Zoyland for much longer in fact, for it moved on to Fairwood Common in July. It was replaced by 222 Squadron which returned to Weston Zoyland on 8 July 1946, having re-equipped with the Gloster Meteor III jet fighter. The unit remained at Weston Zoyland until 1 October, when it moved on to Tangmere. Another unit visited Weston Zoyland during the same period. 151 Squadron arrived on the same day as 222 Squadron, flying its Mosquito NF30 night fighters from Exeter. It is possible that the two squadrons used their time at Weston Zoyland to train together or to develop tactics. The Mosquitos departed on 10 October for Leuchars.

Following the departure of 151 Squadron, Weston Zoyland was unoccupied, and was put onto a Care and Maintenance footing. It remained unused for a few years, until it was hurriedly reopened during the Korean War. A new flying training unit, 209 Advanced Flying School, was opened there on 23 June 1952, to train qualified pilots on the Meteor T7 and F4. The unit was retitled 12 Flying Training School on 1 June 1954, adding Percival Prentices to its inventory, and was closed down on 24 June 1955.

Towards the end of 1955 Canberra jet bombers arrived at Weston Zoyland. The airfield was probably chosen for its somewhat isolated location, as high security was required because the air element of an atomic test monitoring force began forming there for the first British atomic bomb trials in Australia. Canberra B2s of 76 Squadron flew in from Hemswell, to be prepared for the sampling of atomic cloud dispersals, and Canberra PR3s of 542 Squadron arrived from Wyton for high level photographic monitoring. Having made their preparations and undertaken suitable training, the Canberras left for Pearce, Australia in March 1956.

Weston Zoyland's control tower, still standing and seen in July 2005. (Author)

The last units to fly from Weston Zoyland were 32 and 73 Squadrons. Re-roled from fighter-bomber to bomber units, they formed a detachment at Weston Zoyland in January 1957 with 231 Operational Conversion Unit, to train crews on the Canberra B2. At the end of March they departed, flying the Canberras to their new base at Akrotiri in Cyprus.

The station was closed in January 1958, although it was retained as government property until 1969, when the land was sold off for agriculture. The main A372 road was returned to almost its previous route, using part of the main runway. A few buildings including the control tower remain, albeit in a state of dereliction. Substantial parts of the runways also remain in place and are in use by a microlight flying club, providing some echoes of the airfield's past.

11
WHITCHURCH

2 miles south of Bristol
ST 595686

In the late 1920s the Bristol and Wessex Aeroplane Club was looking for a new home, as its base at Filton was becoming very busy. A potential site for a new airfield had been found two miles west of the village of Whitchurch, to the south of Bristol, and in a far-sighted move Bristol City Council, which had been approached by the club, agreed to purchase 298 acres there to establish not only a new home for the aeroplane club but also a purpose-built airport for the city. The area was cleared and levelled, and construction began in 1929. Towards the middle of the following year the work was substantially complete, and on 31 May 1930 Bristol Airport was officially opened by HRH Prince George, Duke of Kent.

A clubhouse had been built for the aeroplane club, along with a public hangar and aircraft sales showroom. The first commercial flights from Whitchurch were air taxi and charter aircraft services, provided by such local companies as Norman Edgar Ltd, which started Bristol Air Taxis Ltd, flying Dessoutter aircraft. Traffic developed slowly but steadily during the 1930s, passenger numbers increasing from a few hundred in 1931 to over 4,000 in 1939. Scheduled passenger services had started in September 1931, initially by Norman Edgar as an extension of their air taxi services. As Western Airways, the company continued to operate from Whitchurch throughout the 1930s, although during that time they moved their main operating base to Weston-super-Mare. They were joined at Whitchurch in 1934 by Imperial Airways, which operated a service for Great Western Railways, and the following year by Railway Air Services and Crilly Airways. These airlines flew mainly the reliable de Havilland biplane twins, the Dragon and Dragon Rapide, with the exception of Imperial Airways/GWR which operated the Westland Wessex trimotor. Among the aircraft operated by Railways Air Services from Whitchurch during the summer of 1935 was a brand new de Havilland Dragon, G-ADDI. It was in this aircraft that the author made his first flight, around Blackpool Tower in 1960. After a long and chequered career in the UK, at the time of writing the aircraft was still flying in the USA.

In July 1935, a new terminal building, called the Main Traffic Hall, was opened, and a couple of months later work began on a Marconi-Adcock direction finding station. This consisted of a transmitter building, a receiver building, and four 80 foot masts, that were erected to the north. On the airfield itself lighting

Aerial view of Whitchurch airport in about 1936. (Aeroplane)

including Chance floodlights, obstruction lights and an illuminated direction indicator was installed, meaning that the airport could be used at night and in bad weather. The apron for receiving and parking aircraft was extended in April 1937, a meteorological office was opened the following month, and in July 104 acres of Court Farm were purchased to allow extension of the airport to the south and east.

Scheduled passenger services from Whitchurch expanded and by the summer of 1938 extended from Liverpool to Penzance. The airport had also been used for recreation and training by the Bristol and Wessex Aeroplane Club, but in 1935 its operations took a new turn when it was approved by the Air Ministry Civil Air Guard programme. The scheme provided for the build-up of a reserve of pilots for use in time of war and under it the government provided a subsidy. The club began CAG training in October 1938, having purchased more aircraft and taken on more flying instructors to meet the huge demand.

Tiger Moths were flown at Whitchurch by 33 E&RFTS and later by 2 Ferry Pool and BOAC. (Author)

Ansons were operated from the airport by 33 E&RFTS and later by 2 Ferry Pool and BOAC. (Aeroplane)

Also that year, another organization increased its use of the airport. Whitchurch had been used for RAF flying training since early 1937, when No. 2 Elementary and Reserve Flying Training School, based at Filton, started utilizing the airfield as a Relief Landing Ground. This use was extended when the Air Ministry negotiated the opening of 33 E&RFTS at the airport. The school opened on 3 December 1938, under a contractual arrangement with Charmier Gilbert Lodge & Co. Ltd. Twelve de Havilland Tiger Moths were operated by the school for elementary flying training, and these were supplemented by Hawker Audax and Hind trainers for advanced flying training and Avro Ansons for Observer/Navigator and Wireless/Observer training.

A hangar, huts and workshops were erected to provide more accommodation for the school during the spring of 1939. However, the international situation deteriorated over the summer, and, with war imminent, Whitchurch was requisitioned by the Air Ministry on 30 August. A couple of days later, on 1 September, aircraft of

British Airways and Imperial Airways began to arrive at the airport. They had been flown to Whitchuch, code-named 'A Base', under a scheme to evacuate the aeroplanes from their operating bases at Croydon and Heston, which were seen as obvious targets for the German Air Force. The airlines were in fact in the process of being merged to become a single, nationalized airline, the British Overseas Airways Corporation, and it was decided to establish the HQ of the new organization at Whitchurch.

At the declaration of war on 3 September 1939, there were over 60 large passenger aircraft parked around the airfield at Whitchurch, including the four-engined Armstrong Whitworth AW27 Ensign (Imperial Airways E Class) and the de Havilland DH91 Albatross (F Class), the Handley Page HP42 biplane (H Class), and British Airways twin-engined Lockheed Electras and Junkers JU52 tri-motors. Whitchurch became the airline's main land plane base, and Poole Harbour its main flying boat base. The technical and administrative staff of Imperial and British Airways were also transferred to Whitchurch.

Until suitable hangar accommodation could be provided, maintenance work had to take place outside. One of the first tasks that had to be undertaken was to camouflage the aircraft, as their natural aluminium finish made them stand out. Soon the graceful shapes of the de Havilland and Armstrong Whitworth airliners were covered in drab green and brown matt camouflage paint. Camouflage was later standardized, but some of the initial schemes painted on by the crews were rather unconventional, such as the sheep painted on the upper wings of an HP42, to give the impression of farmers' fields! BOAC became the basis of National Air Communications, an organization set up to perform essential air transport tasks in time of war. It began scheduled services to France in support of the British Expeditionary Force, often also using other airfields such as Heston, Shoreham and Exeter, but returning to Whitchurch for servicing and maintenance. The aircraft flown were mainly the AW27, DH91 and HP42. Personnel, freight, ammunition and newspapers were soon being regularly carried on these services.

The outbreak of war brought other changes at Whitchurch. There was a ban on all civil flying in the UK apart from authorized flights. All privately owed aircraft had to be registered with the authorities

HP42 and DH91 Albatross, operated by Imperial Airways, shown at Croydon in 1939 just before being withdrawn to Whitchurch. (Aeroplane)

and most were later commandeered by the government for the duration of the war. Under a planned reorganization of RAF flying training, 33 E&RFTS was disbanded and its aircraft were reassigned to other schools. Whitchurch was declared a restricted area and barbed wire fences were erected along its perimeter. Its buildings were camouflaged, and the road running along the eastern boundary was closed to unauthorized vehicles. Pillboxes were later built around the airfield, the defences being manned by a Home Guard unit formed from BOAC staff.

The opening of hostilities also created a need for more aircraft for the RAF and Fleet Air Arm. These were being steadily produced by the aircraft manufacturers, but needed to be ferried between the factory airfields, the Aircraft Storage Units, and the operational squadrons. With the demand for operational pilots by the RAF, there was a shortage of pilots for other duties such as ferrying. The

RAF pilots that were available were organized into ferry pools, and they were soon supplemented by civilian volunteer pilots from the Air Transport Auxiliary. This organization made use of the many civilian pilots that had been grounded, and the many women pilots who were unable to fly with the services. When use of the ATA in the ferrying role was proposed to the Air Ministry, they were sceptical. In September 1939 an initial batch of 30 candidate pilots was gathered at Whitchurch to undertake flying tests on Airspeed Couriers. Many of the male candidates were accepted for ferry duties with the ATA, and they were soon joined by a number of female pilots. A large proportion of the ATA pilots went on to be trained to fly military aircraft at the Central Flying School, Upavon.

The ATA was officially formed as an operational organization on 1 January 1940, with its headquarters at White Waltham in Berkshire. Although the selection of potential ATA pilots was also transferred from Whitchurch to White Waltham, in February 1940 the ATA School was set up at Whitchurch. This provided advanced training to pilots selected for the ATA, using Avro Tutor, Miles Magister, and North American Harvard single-engined tandem

Lockheed Electra, flown by British Airways from the airport. (Aeroplane)

trainers, and also the twin-engined Bristol Blenheim Mk I. ATA ferry pools were set up around the country, usually at airfields near to aircraft manufacturers' factories. Eventually there were to be 22 such ATA ferry pools, as far apart as Hamble near Southampton, Belfast in Northern Ireland, and Lossiemouth in northern Scotland. Their tasks were co-ordinated by Central Ferry Control, set up at Andover in Hampshire.

On 15 February 1940, B Section of No. 3 Ferry Pilots Pool (ATA) was formed at Whitchurch in order to provide a pool of pilots, mainly to ferry aircraft produced by the Bristol Aircraft Co. at Filton. The importance of this task was confirmed on 5 November 1940 when B Section was redesignated a pool in its own right: No. 2 Ferry Pilots Pool (ATA). The primary task of the pool was the delivery of Bristol Blenheims, Beauforts and Beaufighters from Filton, Hawker Hurricanes built by Gloster aircraft at Hucclecote, and later Supermarine Spitfires and Westland Whirlwinds manufactured by Westland Aircraft at Yeovil and Beaufighters from the shadow factory at Old Mixon, Weston-super-Mare. The unit had a number of aircraft on strength, primarily to act as

AW27 Ensign flown by Imperial Airways into Whitchurch during September 1939, and later in camouflage operated from the airport. (Aeroplane)

airborne taxis to take the pilots to the airfields that they needed to get to in order to collect aircraft, but also to provide experience of a variety of aircraft types. The pool at Whitchurch was eventually to have the use of Bristol Beaufort, Hawker Hurricane, Curtiss Mohawk, Miles Monospar, DH89 Dominie, Miles Magister, Avro Anson, Supermarine Spitfire, and Bristol Beaufighter. The ATA pilots moved trainer aircraft to start with, but as official confidence in their capabilities grew, they moved on to fighters, light bombers, transports, and eventually heavy bombers. Depending on their level of experience and training, later in the war ATA pilots could be called upon to ferry any one of 147 different aircraft types. Their only guidance was their experience and a thin volume entitled *Ferry Pilots Notes*, which gave each aircraft's basic characteristics and operating details. From the original 28 pilots recruited at Whitchurch in September 1939, the number of ATA pilots rose to 650 five years later. In total over 309,000 aircraft were ferried by ATA pilots during the Second World War, and 173 pilots and eight flight engineers lost their lives on ATA service.

BOAC formally came into being on 1 April 1940, but losses to its fleet had already started to occur. A gale at Whitchurch on 19 March blew HP42s G-AAVD *Hanno* and G-AAXC *Hercules* together, damaging them beyond repair. Then followed the loss of two Ensigns during the Battle of France, and an accident to a third shortly afterwards.

Arrivals at Whitchurch during the summer of 1940 included eight Sabena (Belgian Airlines) aircraft and six of KLM Royal Dutch Airlines, following the German invasion of Belgium and Holland. The Belgian aircraft soon moved on to the Congo, but the KLM aircraft, a Douglas DC-2 and five DC-3s, were later operated under charter to BOAC. Another escapee during this time was Danish Airlines' Focke Wulf FW 200B Condor OY-DAM *Dania*. Like the Dutch aircraft it was painted a bright orange finish signifying neutrality, but it was soon camouflaged. Having been earmarked as a potential escape aircraft for the Dutch royal family to fly to Canada, the Condor was fitted with long range tanks and registered as G-AGAY. It was later painted in RAF markings as DX177, and issued to the ATA.

On 6 June 1940 BOAC inaugurated a new international route, to Heston and then to Lisbon, using DH91s, which connected to

Focke-Wulfe FW200 Condor of Danish Air Lines, sister ship of OY-DAM that escaped to Whitchurch during the summer of 1940. (Aeroplane)

services to the Middle East, South Africa and beyond, using a mixed fleet of land planes and flying boats. Later the DC-2s and DC-3s of KLM replaced the DH91s on the Lisbon run, using Whitchurch as their base. The Dutch crews and aircraft were to maintain a safe and efficient service on this very difficult and dangerous route. There was a near loss on 21 September 1940, when DC-3 G-AGBC was badly damaged while landing at Whitchurch in fog. The aircraft struck an anti-glider pole on approach and crashed. However, there were no passengers aboard, and no crew members were injured.

Notwithstanding the intense flying activity at Whitchurch, its flight safety was good. That is not to say, of course, that accidents did not occur. For example DH91 G-ACDL *Fingal*, crashed on 6 October shortly after departure from Whitchurch, when all four engines failed owing to a fuel system fault. The aircraft's captain managed to bring it down skilfully near Pucklechurch, clipping a cottage in the process. The aircraft was a write-off, but none of the crew or passengers was injured. A further loss occurred a few days later when DH91 G-ACDI *Frobisher*, the flagship of the fleet, was destroyed at Whitchurch in an arson attack by a disgruntled former employee. On 16 October, two RAF Hurricanes visiting Whitchurch were damaged. The flight of three aircraft of 504 Squadron had been scrambled from Filton, but couldn't locate its intended quarry. Unable then to find their base in the deteriorating weather, the aircraft located Whitchurch. The first landed successfully, but the second nosed over on landing, and the third overran through the southern boundary hedge and ended up in a pond.

Despite the difficulties, a good level of service was maintained from Whitchurch. In October 1940, for example, 40 services were flown to and from Lisbon, carrying 272 passengers, 7,586 kgs of freight and 11,710 kgs of mail. However, further aircraft losses occurred the following month. The Bristol area had become an important target for the Luftwaffe, and the city and its docks suffered many raids during the autumn and winter of 1940. A heavy raid occurred during the night of 24 November, when Whitchurch was attacked. Incendiary and high explosive bombs were dropped on the airport, resulting in the destruction of Ensign G-ADTC *Endymion* and the KLM DC-3 G-AGBO *Wulp*. Three Ensigns were damaged by splinters and shrapnel, along with the Condor G-AGAY and DC-3 G-AGGB. However, the damaged aircraft were soon repaired and put back into service.

In the spring of 1941 the Bristol Aircraft Company (BAC) started using the south site for the assembly and storage of Beaufighter Mk II night fighters. These aircraft were fitted with the Rolls-Royce Merlin XX engine, but, as the powerplant was also fitted to the new Avro Lancaster four-engined bomber, supplies were short. As the Merlins became available they were fitted into the stored Beaufighters, which were then flight-tested at the airport before being ferried away by the ATA. A large factory building, a Bellman hangar, two smaller hangars, and several outbuildings on the south site were later used by BAC as an engine overhaul works. Also on this site were the control tower, and airport administration and passenger reception buildings. In addition, Bristol had use of a hangar on the north site for stores (later also used by the University Air Squadron). This site also accommodated the BOAC, KLM and

Luftwaffe target photograph of Bristol (Whitchurch) Airport, taken during the summer of 1940. (Nigel J Clarke Publications)

ATA offices and workshops, a T2 hangar, shared by BOAC and KLM, and a Bellman, used by ATA. Further hangars were built later, and eventually five occupied the north site.

On 4 July 1941 a new service was started by BOAC from Whitchurch. This was to Dublin, to link up with a new BOAC flying-boat service to the USA using Boeing 314As. DH91 Albatrosses were used on the service, which was switched to a new airport , later known as Shannon Airport, built next to the flying boat terminal at Foynes.

The increased use of Whitchurch by heavy aircraft had resulted in rutting of the surface, so it was decided to lay a new concrete and tarmac runway, along with taxiways to link it to the hangars and aprons to the north and south. Work had started earlier in 1941, the eastern taxiways having been laid in July. Eventually, in November, the main runway, with a length of 3,048 feet and a width of 150 feet, was complete. A taxiway at the runway's western end linked it to the north side. The other runways remained grass-surfaced, but were reinforced and regraded. (One, from south-east to north-west, was 3,060 feet long, and the other, from north-east to south-west, was 2,870 feet.)

As Britain's main gateway to the rest of the free world for civil traffic, Whitchurch played an important part in the Second World War that was never publicized at the time for security reasons. In the press it was always referred to as 'a West Country Airport', as on the occasion of the arrival of the US Ambassador, J.G. Winnant in March 1941. He flew from the USA to Lisbon by US airline and then by KLM DC-3 to Whitchurch.

BOAC was always hard pressed to provide its services with the small fleet of aircraft that it had at its disposal. Although it gained some 50 aircraft during the first two years of the war, it had lost about 20 during that time. As well as Lockheed Lodestars, the government also provided three ex-RAF Consolidated Liberators in September 1941 for the Atlantic return ferry service. By the end of 1941 BOAC had a 63-strong fleet of 27 flying boats and 36 landplanes. Some of these were based overseas (many of the Lodestars, for example, operated on African routes), and, although most of the UK-based aircraft used Whitchurch for maintenance, some operated from other bases such as Lyneham, from which the Liberators flew. In early 1942 the aircraft based at Whitchurch included six Ensigns, three DH91s, the DC-3s of KLM, and the prototype Curtiss Wright CW-20, a twin-engined 24 seat passenger and cargo aircraft that was the forerunner of the Curtiss C-46 Commando. Registered as G-AGDI, the CW-20 flew services to Gibraltar in the spring of 1942, and from May was also used on a night service from Gibraltar to Malta.

Of the many international passengers arriving at Whitchurch during the spring of 1942, the group that stepped off the KLM DC-3 from Lisbon on 20 February was particularly notable, comprising

Brigadier General Ira C. Eaker of the US Army Air Force and his staff. The party immediately left for London, where they would present plans to the government for the arrival of the US Eighth Air Force, a powerful strategic bomber force that would join RAF Bomber Command in the Allied air offensive against Germany. Other visitors that month included HRH Duke of Kent, who met representatives of the Air Ministry, BOAC, KLM and 2 Ferry Pilots Pool (which was redesignated 2 Ferry Pool on 1 May 1942).

Some Armstrong Whitworth Whitley Vs arrived at Whitchurch in April. They were the first of a batch of the twin-engined bombers that had been converted as freighters for BOAC. Following proving flights to West Africa, 13 aircraft went into service, flying from Whitchurch to Lagos, Gibraltar, and sometimes to Shannon. They were also later used between Leuchars and Stockholm, and for the night run from Gibraltar to Malta until replaced by Lockheed Hudsons in August 1942. Only one Whitley was lost in BOAC service: G-AGCI crashed into the sea off Gibraltar on 26 September 1942, killing Captain C.G.K. Browne and his crew of three.

Part of the organization established by BOAC at Whitchurch was the airline's Central Training School, which undertook type conversion, refresher training, and other aircrew training tasks such as instrument flying training. The school maintained the skills of existing pilots, but also trained new arrivals, mainly aircrew on secondment from the RAF's Bomber and Coastal Commands. When available, Dakotas were provided for training as required, along with four Airspeed Oxfords that were on loan from the RAF. Later, towards the end of 1944, the CTS fleet would consist of six Oxfords and two Dakotas.

Virtually every type of landplane and amphibian in service with the RAF and FAA passed through Whitchurch during the war years. Most of these were in the hands of the ATA pilots, flying through in transit from aircraft factory to maintenance units, RAF units, or other ferry pools. They ranged in size from Auster single-engined Army Co-operation light-planes to Lancaster four-engined bombers. Rare types such as the Curtiss Mohawk and Bell Airacobra mingled with other types that were still on the secret list, such as the Westland Whirlwind and Hawker Typhoon. Frequent visitors were in-service RAF aircraft such as the Airspeed Oxfords and Miles Masters from the flying training station at Lulsgate

Masters (here shown in Mark I and Mark III versions) were flown by the ATA from Whitchurch. (Aeroplane)

Bottom (which eventually became Bristol Airport, replacing Whitchurch). RAF trainers became resident at Whitchurch once more from 20 July 1942, when Tiger Moths of the Bristol University Air Squadron, based at Filton, were detached to fly from the airport to give pre-entry flying experience to university students about to join the RAF.

KLM extended its Whitchurch-Lisbon route on 15 October 1942 with two flights per week to Gibraltar. However, this period of the war coincided with a build-up of German long-range fighter patrols trying to prevent RAF Coastal Command aircraft from attacking U-boats in the Bay of Biscay and the Western Approaches. This activity posed a real threat to civil traffic passing through the area, such as the KLM flights, and on 15 November DC-3 G-AGBB *Ibis* was attacked over the Bay of Biscay by a lone German fighter. Although the DC-3 was hit, its pilot managed to evade the enemy aircraft by flying into cloud. The DC-3 was attacked a second time on 19 April 1943, when it was intercepted and fired at by three Messerschmitt Bf110s. The pilot dived the DC-3 to sea level and made good his escape. Although the aircraft had a few bullet holes in it, the passengers, who included the Assistant British Air Attaché to Portugal, were unhurt. Unfortunately G-AGBB's luck ran out on 1 June when it was returning to Whitchurch; three hours out from Lisbon, the aircraft's pilot Captain Quirinus Tepas, OBE, KLM's chief pilot, radioed to say that he was being attacked. The DC-3 had been intercepted by a patrol of eight JU88C-6 long range fighters of KG40, based at Bordeaux-Meignac, which shot the defenceless airliner down into the sea. As well as the captain, four crew members and 13 passengers died, including Hollywood actor Leslie Howard.

Because of this disastrous incident, the Lisbon service was flown at night only. The BOAC aircraft were fitted with flame-damping exhausts and astro-navigation domes, and, until the KLM aircraft could be modified with these essential night-flying aids, they were withdrawn from the service. In the meantime BOAC increased its Lisbon flights to four per week, at night, using Dakotas, six of which had been transferred from the RAF earlier in the year. Refuelling stops were made when necessary at Chivenor, Portreath or Trebelzue when heading south, and at Opporto when northbound. A new service was introduced during the summer of 1943, to Fez, and later Rabat in northern Morocco, using Dakotas. At first the aircraft departed from Lyneham and returned to Whitchurch but later Whitchurch also became the departure airport. Another 14 Dakotas had been received by BOAC towards the end of the year, and the airline's wartime fleet eventually totalled 130 aircraft.

The summer of 1943 saw the last of the DH91s. These aircraft had kept up services between Whitchurch and Shannon, but were getting more difficult to maintain. The final flight was made on 6 July by G-AFDK *Fortuna*. The aircraft took off from Whitchurch with eight senior members of BOAC aboard. Unfortunately, as it approached Shannon, the aircraft did not live up to its name, as one of its flaps separated from the wing and smashed into the tail. The pilot, Captain G.P. Moss, was forced to put the DH91 down on the nearest suitable piece of ground, which was a mud flat in the river estuary. Although the aircraft was wrecked, only one of the occupants, a passenger, was slightly hurt. The remaining two DH91s were grounded at Whitchurch pending an accident investigation, but were in any case scrapped a couple of months later.

Dakotas replaced the DH91s, and from 4 August BOAC started a twice-weekly Whitchurch-Gibraltar service, followed by a weekly Whitchurch-Madrid-Lisbon service on 24 October. Towards the end of November a further service, to Algiers, was inaugurated. Following a refuelling stop at St Mawgan/Trebelzue the aircraft (Dakotas) flew to Gibraltar before landing at Algiers. The return flight was via Rabat to Gibraltar. For ease of identification, the aircraft were painted with full RAF Transport Command markings and, for their protection, the BOAC crew wore RAF uniforms, as they were operating in areas that had only recently come under Allied control.

Among the many visitors to Whitchurch in 1943 were several aircraft of the USAAF, including P-47 Thunderbolts with engine trouble and, on 23 September, two B-17 Flying Fortresses. The aircraft were from the 91st Bombardment Group, based at Bassingbourn, and had run low on fuel while returning from a raid on Nantes. They refuelled on the north side apron and were able to continue their return to base. However, a B-24 Liberator that arrived shortly afterwards with technical problems was fully fuelled and bombed up. The aircraft was unloaded and dismantled for its return to base by road. Other US arrivals included Stinson L-5 Sentinel liaison aircraft, several of which were based at Whitchurch from October 1943 onwards as communications aircraft for the First US Army, which had established its HQ at Clifton College, Bristol. They were to become a familiar sight over the following months.

RAF aircraft still visited. Unfortunately two such aircraft came to grief at Whitchurch early in 1944, both of them Oxfords from 3 Flying Instructors' School (Advanced), based at Lulsgate Bottom. On 15 February LW776 crashed just after take-off from Whitchurch when both engines cut out at 300 feet. The aircraft then stalled and hit the ground, killing both occupants, Flight Lieutenant Garvey and Flying Officer L.W.R. Rogers. On 23 March Oxford HN203 suffered an engine failure during an overshoot and crash landed. Although the aircraft was a write-off, the two crew members escaped uninjured. Most other visitors passing through Whitchurch during 1943 and 1944 arrived safely. Amongst them were many VIPs and entertainers, the former including Queen Wilhelmina of the Netherlands, the Prime Minister Winston Churchill, and Mrs Eleanor Roosevelt, wife of the US President, and the latter Bob Hope, Bing Crosby, Dinah Shore and Edward G. Robinson.

The KLM flights to Lisbon and Gibraltar with DC-3s were resumed on 29 March 1944, and on 18 April G-AGBD *Buizerd* completed KLM's 1,000th return service to Lisbon for BOAC. On 16 April BOAC started a service to West Africa with Dakotas. After stopping at St Mawgan to top up on fuel the aircraft then flew Lisbon – Rabat – Port Etienne – Dakar – Bathurst – Freetown – Takkoradi – Accra – Lagos. Occasionally stops were also made at Abingdon. This punishing 23-day round trip was not popular with the crews, however. Other services, such as to Cairo and Karachi were more popular, and not so time-consuming.

Due to activity at the US Army HQ at Clifton, the level of visiting USAAF aircraft increased during 1944, as the build-up to the invasion of Normandy began. Light transports such as the single-engined Fairchild UC-61A Forwarder and Noorduyn UC-64 Norseman and the twin-engined Cessna UC-78 Bobcat were seen, as well as Douglas C-47 Skytrains (the US military version of the Dakota). More frequent visitors, however, were the Piper L-4 Cub and Stinson L-5 Sentinel light communications aircraft of the liaison squadrons that brought staff to conferences, mail, and despatches. Several aircraft of the 153rd Liaison Squadron were based at Whitchurch, sharing one of the BAC hangars on the south side. HQ First Army and the 153rd Liaison Squadron moved onto the Continent after D-Day, and they were replaced by HQ Ninth US Army and 125th Liaison Squadron. (By the end of August they too had gone to France.) One of the L-5 Sentinels was involved in a flying accident at Whitchurch on 10 July 1944 when it collided with a Miles Magister of 3 FIS(A). Both aircraft were approaching to land, but apparently neither pilot saw the other. The aircraft crashed to the ground and burnt out, but both occupants of each aircraft survived, although injured.

Despite the momentous events taking place on the Continent following the invasion, passenger and freight services continued uninterrupted from Whitchurch. The BOAC UK–Algiers service was extended to Cairo from 27 June. Dakotas were flown on this route, and the aircraft was proving itself to be a reliable workhorse. Accidents were few, but as a reminder of what can happen, G-AGIR, one of the Whitchurch-based Dakotas, was lost on 28 August when it crashed at Telmest in the Atlas Mountains near Casablanca. The pilot, Captain L.J.M. White, four crew and three passengers were killed.

A new service to Whitchurch was started on 17 September 1944 when a Lockheed Lodestar of the Belgian airline Sabena arrived from Léopoldville in the Belgian Congo (which had been Sabena's base since 1940), having flown via Lagos, Kano, Aoulef, Casablanca and Lisbon. The Lodestar took off on its return trip a week later. The service continued until May 1945, when it was switched to newly-liberated Brussels. On 9 October 1944 daylight flights to and from Lisbon were resumed, and a more direct route was now followed, the wide detour around the Bay of Biscay no longer being required. The first direct flight to Madrid took place by Dakota a few weeks later, on 23 October. Shortly afterwards flights to Le Bourget, Paris started from Whitchurch, also by Dakota.

In November 1944 the first of a batch of 23 Dakota IV aircraft arrived at Whitchurch, bringing the number of Dakotas based at Whitchurch to 57. Although many of these operated from other stations, the engineering branch based at Whitchurch was responsible for their technical upkeep. The Whitchurch engineering branch also looked after other aircraft, such as the BOAC Lockheed Hudsons and Lodestars based at Leuchars and Cairo, which came in for major maintenance and Certificate of Airworthiness inspections. The overall size of the BOAC fleet had increased from 109 landplanes and flying boats on 1 January 1943 to 140 aircraft in January 1945. About 40 per cent of the aircraft were based at Whitchurch, but this was soon to change, as a new main UK operations base for BOAC had been set up towards the end of 1944 at Hurn near Bournemouth. One of the reasons for this was that Hurn's runways were long enough to take BOAC's large four-engined Liberators and the new transport versions of the Lancaster (the York and the Lancastrian) that were coming into service. With the liberation of the Netherlands, KLM ceased their operations from Whitchurch on 31 December and transferred to

Dakotas were operated from Whitchurch by BOAC and as the C-47 by the USAAF. (Aeroplane)

Holland. BOAC started a replacement service from Hurn to Gibraltar.

As 1945 moved on, BOAC activity from Whitchurch gradually reduced. With the end of the war in Europe there was a decline too in ATA activity, and in September No. 2 Ferry Pool closed. In June 1945, the Air Ministry had transferred control of Whitchurch Airport to the Ministry of Civil Aviation, who then assumed responsibility for air traffic control and other support and technical services. BOAC continued to use Whitchurch for training until 1946, when it transferred this activity to the new Central Training School at Aldermaston, Berkshire (later to become Airways Training Ltd). Dakota activity reduced with the transfer of 19 Dakotas and support staff to Northolt, where BOAC's European Division was to be set up (later to become British European Airways [BEA]). However, Whitchurch remained an active airport, with 14 Dakota services operating weekly, including long-haul flights to Cairo and West Africa.

Post-war civil flying from Whitchurch was slow to get off the ground. In July 1946 Great Western and Southern Airlines started scheduled flights to Cardiff and Southampton, using DH Dragon Rapides, but the following year the airline was nationalized and absorbed into BEA, who closed the routes, as they were considered uneconomical. The Bristol and Wessex Aeroplane Club reopened with three Taylorcraft Austers and despite fuel rationing managed to recruit a good number of members. In August 1946 all remaining Dakota scheduled services from Whitchurch were transferred to other airports and, although Dakota maintenance was to continue for a couple of years more, in 1948 BOAC aircraft finally left, on transfer to the airline's new operating base at Heathrow. A BOAC presence remained at Whitchurch in the form of a Technical Training School stores depot, and the newly formed Bristol branch of the Airways Flying Club, which flew a variety of types including Miles Hawk Trainers (a civilian version of the Magister).

In 1950 scheduled services restarted from Whitchurch with the introduction of flights to the Channel Islands by Moreton Air Services, using Airspeed Consuls, and in May the following year Aer Lingus introduced a DC-3 service to Dublin. Services from Whitchurch increased over the next few years, with Cambrian Air Services taking over Moreton's routes, using Rapides, and then DH Doves, Herons, and Dakotas. However, during the mid 1950s more and more houses were being built in the Whitchurch area, and, because of this and the limited expansion potential of Whitchurch, it was finally decided to close the airfield and transfer all remaining activity to the new Bristol Airport at Lulsgate Bottom.

Flying officially came to an end at Whitchurch on 13 April 1957. Unofficially, several aircraft flew into Whitchurch over the following years, using the airfield's runway for emergency landings. At the time of writing, the last landing at Whitchurch was on 10 November 1993, when a Cessna 152 en route to Lulsgate landed because of a fuel problem. Aviation activity went on at Whitchurch after closure of the airport, as the Bristol Aeroplane Co. continued the maintenance of aero-engines in its north side premises until 1971, when the work was transferred to Patchway. The hangars were later incorporated into an industrial estate built on the site, and other, more recent, developments include a sports centre and leisure park. Today's users of the area and its facilities are probably unaware of the important role that Whitchurch played during the Second World War, and that it was the site not only of Bristol's first airport but also one of the first civil airports in the country.

12
YEOVIL

1 mile south-west of Yeovil
ST 540158

Yeovil airfield was established in April 1915 as the site for the Westland aircraft works by the Yeovil engineering firm Petters Ltd. This event occurred almost overnight, as the direct result of a speech made in the House of Commons by the Prime Minister, David Lloyd George. He questioned the suitability of the munitions available for carrying on the war. Upon hearing of this, Ernest Petter, the managing director of Petters Ltd, convened a board meeting and passed a resolution by which the company placed their manufacturing resources at the disposal of the government to make anything that they called for. The next day the board were called to a conference at the Admiralty and offered a contract to build Short 184 seaplanes. Although supplying aeroplanes was hardly what the Petters directors had expected, they got to work immediately. Because the Petters foundry was in the centre of Yeovil, the company had purchased additional land out of town in 1913 as part of an expansion scheme. It was planned to build a new foundry at West Handford, to the west of Yeovil, and, because of its location, Mrs Petter chose the name Westland for the proposed new development, which also included a garden village to house the workforce. It was decided to use this land for aeroplane manufacture. Although wholly owned by Petters, it was felt that the new venture ought to be kept apart from the main oil-engine manufacturing company, and so the Westland Aircraft Works was set up as a separate company.

The Westland Aircraft Company works seen from the air in July 1930. (Aeroplane)

Despite the daunting challenge, Petters got stuck in, extending the factory and bringing in experienced people. Eight months later, the first aeroplane was finished! On completion, the first batch of aircraft was crated up and delivered to the Royal Naval Air Service stations at Rochester and Hamble for flight test and acceptance. This arrangement was all very well for floatplanes such as the Short 184, but clearly impractical if the company wanted to make landplanes. Early in 1917, therefore, land was purchased alongside the factory for an airfield, so that the aircraft could be flight-tested on site and delivered by air if necessary. With the contract for Short seaplanes completed, another, for Sopwith One-and-a-half Strutter landplanes, followed.

181

By this time the factory was also making Air Co. DH4s, and in April the first aircraft was flight-tested before being delivered from Yeovil directly to the Western Front. DH9s followed, and the company started to get involved in development work when it was asked to fit the DH9 with the US Liberty engine. This was the DH9A, one of the outstanding aircraft of the Great War. When the Armistice came the factory had manufactured 1,100 aircraft for the RNAS, RFC and RAF. The last of these were huge Vickers Vimy twin-engined bombers, for which the company had built a new erecting shop with an unsupported roof span of 140 feet (at the time the largest building of its kind in Britain).

After the war, the company retained a contract from the Air Ministry to build more DH9As, and spares to support them in service. With the backing of the parent company, Westland therefore decided to stay in the aviation business, and in the lean years that lay ahead DH9A work provided business for Westlands. In the hope that a production order would follow, the company produced a string of prototypes during this time – including the Weasel two-seat fighter, Limousine light passenger transport, Walrus carrier-based spotter, Dreadnought mailplane, Woodpigeon light biplane, Widgeon light monoplane, Yeovil bomber, Westbury fighter, and Wizard fighter. Success eventually came in 1927 with an order for the Wapiti, a bomber and general purpose biplane, to replace the DH9A, which was then in service with the RAF all over the Empire. The fact that the Wapiti incorporated a large number of DH9A components was probably a major factor in deciding the Air Ministry competition in Westland's favour!

The company was to build 563 Wapitis, which gave long service in India, Iraq, South Africa, and the UK; at one time in the 1930s, the RAF had more Wapitis in service than any other type. More designs followed during the 1930s, some successful and some not. These included the Witch bomber, Pterodactyl research aircraft, Westland IV transport, Wessex transport, F20/27 interceptor, COW gun fighter, PV7 torpedo bomber, and F7/30 fighter. The company also developed a number of private venture designs based on the Waipiti, including the Westland-Houston PV3, two examples of which flew over the summit of Mount Everest (29,030 feet) in 1930, establishing a world altitude record. The company made a brief excursion into rotary-winged aircraft in 1936, building two Cierva designs, the CL-20 and CL-29 autogyros.

The company's name had changed to the Westland Aircraft Company in 1934, when Teddy Petter, Sir Ernest's son, became the technical director. Under his leadership the company submitted a design for an army co-operation aircraft to replace the Audax. The company's hard work in preparing this design paid off when they were awarded an Air Ministry contract for two prototypes in June 1935. The first one performed its maiden flight at Boscombe Down on 15 June 1936, and three months later the design entered production as the Lysander. In the meantime, Westland received a sub-contract from Hawker Aircraft to build the Hector, which had been ordered as an interim Audax replacement. Westland built all 178 examples of the type between February and December 1937.

In 1938 control of Petters and of the Westland Aircraft Company passed to John Brown and Co., the Clydeside shipbuilders, and one of their first actions was to build a new erecting shop at Yeovil. Thus when war came in 1939, the company was in a strong

The Wapiti was in production at Yeovil during the 1930s. (Aeroplane)

Westland's successful Lysander design. The 4 Squadron aircraft seen here is picking up a written message. (Aeroplane)

managerial, financial, and technical position. Two aircraft designs were in production at Yeovil when the war started. Of these, the Lysander had entered service with 16 Squadron at Old Sarum in May 1938, and went on to serve with over 30 squadrons and dozens of other RAF units. The aircraft had an excellent short take-off and landing capability, which made it ideal for the role for which it was intended, that of army co-operation. It went to France with four squadrons of the Air Component, British Expeditionary Force, in September 1939 and fought during the Battle of France. It was later replaced in this role by Tomahawks and Mustangs, but it served on target facilities and air-sea rescue work, as well as with special duties units delivering secret agents to occupied Europe. When production finished in January 1942, a total of 1,426 had been made by Westland (a further 225 were built under licence in Canada). The Lysander continued in service with the RAF until November 1945.

The Westland Whirlwind, which first flew in October 1938. (Aeroplane)

As well as the Lysander there was another project in progress at Westlands in 1936. This was the company's response to Specification F37/35, calling for a single-seat heavily-armed day and night fighter. A low-wing twin-engined monoplane was designed by Teddy Petter's team, and the prototype was built under conditions of great secrecy. Although it had been flown from Boscombe Down on 11 October 1938 by the company's chief test pilot, Harald Penrose, it was not until two years later that the existence of the Westland Whirlwind was officially confirmed. The aircraft was fast and highly manoeuvrable, with a potent armament in the form of four 20 mm Hispano cannon in the nose. However, the aircraft had two major shortcomings. One was that, although its engines (Rolls-Royce Peregrines) gave it good low level performance, this tailed off at altitude, and so they would not give the power required at the heights at which wartime combats were then being fought. The other was that the Whirlwind's landing speed was high, preventing its use on short, grass runways. Production orders were therefore cut back, and only 114 aircraft were eventually to be manufactured. The Whirlwind in fact had been the first twin-engined single-seat fighter to enter service anywhere, and it did go on to a successful career as a low-level strike fighter.

Westland's next major project was the design of a high-altitude fighter to meet Air Ministry Specification F7/41. Features called for in the specification included an armament of six 20 mm cannon, provision for airborne interception radar, and, most critically, a pressurized cockpit, as the required service ceiling was set at over 42,000 feet. The Welkin, as the aircraft was to be known, was similar to the Whirlwind in design, but was a mid-wing, not low wing, monoplane, and it had Rolls-Royce Merlin engines installed in its high aspect ratio wings, which spanned 70 feet. One problem

The Welkin high altitude interceptor. (Aeroplane)

Tomahawks were modified by Westlands during 1940/41. (Aeroplane)

area was the pressurized cabin, of which Westlands had no experience. Eventually they were to develop a system whereby the aircraft could fly at heights of 45,000 feet, yet maintain a height of 24,000 feet internally. The pilot was always on oxygen when flying the aircraft, and if pressure was lost by sudden damage to the cabin, the loss would be far less serious than if full pressurization had been maintained. The automatic pressurization valves were developed by part of the firm which later established the Normalair Company, leading manufacturers of cabin pressurization and air conditioning equipment fitted to post-war civil airliners. The Welkin met the design requirements, but by the time of its first flight in November 1942, the threat of high altitude German raiders had largely disappeared. Of the 100 aircraft manufactured, 33 were unfinished, and none went into squadron service. Several aircraft were used in high altitude research programmes, but the majority went into store before being scrapped.

Spitfire IIs and Vs were produced at Yeovil during 1940/41. This is a Mark II. (Author)

As well as designing, developing and manufacturing aircraft of their own, from early in the war Westland also undertook the sub-contracted manufacture, repair and servicing of aircraft built by other companies, British and American. This began with the incorporation of minor modifications in Curtiss Mohawk, Tomahawk and Kittyhawk aircraft, such as the fitting of British radio equipment, and of British instruments in the case of those aircraft that had been diverted from the French Air Force after the French capitulation.

The destruction of the Supermarine factory at Eastleigh by the Luftwaffe brought Spitfire production to a standstill, and the Westland Aircraft Company was asked by the Ministry of Aircraft Production to assist. Within three months Spitfires were rolling off the production line at Yeovil, supported by a network of component suppliers that had been established in the local area. Almost 700 Spitfire IIas, Vs, and Vcs were produced, before the company was asked to assist with the Fairey Barracuda torpedo bomber. However, only 18 Barracudas had been produced by Westland before, because of their Spitfire expertise, they were switched to Seafire work, which was seen as higher priority. They produced an initial batch of the early version of the Seafire, the Mk IIc, which had conventional wings. While this work was in progress, Westland worked with Supermarine to devise a satisfactory wing-folding mechanism to ease storage problems aboard ship. Westland was then made prime-contractor for the Seafire, including Marks IIc, IIIc, XV, and XVII. When it was apparent that the volume involved would exceed the company's production capacity, Westland engaged Cunliffe-Owen Aircraft as their main sub-contractor. The two companies subsequently produced over 2,400 Seafires by the end of the war, Westland producing over 60% of them in their factories in Yeovil and at Ilchester (on Yeovilton's airfield).

It was realized that the intense activity at Yeovil would draw the attention of the Luftwaffe, and so various attempts were made to camouflage the works' airfield. Hedges and ditches were simulated across the landing ground by spraying tar across the grass, and parts of the factory were disguised as rows of houses. Despite this, the Germans made several attempts to bomb the factory. The first attack came on 15 July 1940, when several Junkers JU88 bombers made a surprise raid, diving out of cloud and dropping twelve bombs onto the airfield. They hit one of the flight sheds and cratered the grass, but no other damage was sustained and several Whirlwinds parked beside the factory were untouched. The next attempt was made late in the afternoon of 30 September and involved a much larger force of enemy aircraft. Forty Heinkel He111s of KG55, escorted by Messerschmitt Bf110s, flew across the Dorset coast, heading for Yeovil, but they were intercepted by the Hurricanes of 56 Squadron from Boscombe Down and 504 Squadron at Filton, and by the Spitfires of 152 Squadron, based at Warmwell. The raiders turned away and headed back across the Channel. A more successful raid was made on 7 October 1940, when 25 Junkers JU88s of II/KG51, escorted by 50 Bf110s of ZG26, crossed the coast with Yeovil as their intended target. Although the Germans were once again intercepted by RAF fighter squadrons vectored in by 10 Group and nine of the raiders were shot down, this time they fought their way through to their target. Bombs were

Over 60% of all Seafires were produced at Westland. These Mark Ibs are from 736 Squadron, Yeovilton. (Aeroplane)

dropped, but fortunately only slight damage was sustained by the factory. However, a shelter was hit in the raid, and just over 100 workers inside were injured. Yeovil continued to be a target for the Luftwaffe, and further small-scale raids continued through the winter into 1941. The last of these took place on 26 March 1941, when a lone Dornier Do17, appearing overhead during the middle of the day, dropped bombs, killing one factory worker and injuring several others.

Well before the end of the war Westland was to be involved in its final fixed-wing aircraft project. The Wyvern (design number W34) was originally devised in 1943 as an anti-shipping strike fighter. It was a single-engined, low-wing monoplane, originally with a Rolls-Royce Eagle piston engine driving a contra-rotating propeller, but it was not until 16 December 1946 that the prototype took off on its first flight, from Boscombe Down, with Harald Penrose at the controls. The final and definitive version, fitted with an Armstrong Siddeley Python turboprop engine, was the Wyvern S Mk 4, which was the variant that eventually went into service in May 1953. The production total was 120. The aircraft served with eight squadrons of the Fleet Air Arm, and was used operationally at Suez. The last Wyvern was withdrawn in 1958.

The end of the war meant that Britain's large aircraft industry would have to reduce drastically in size and adapt to peacetime needs. The Westland Aircraft Company did diversify, but the management decided to remain in aviation by concentrating on a new area, that of rotorcraft. This was a bold decision, as the helicopter was still in its infancy. Nonetheless, Westland made up for its lack of experience in the field by teaming up with the US helicopter manufacturers Sikorsky, and negotiated an agreement to build their designs under licence. The first was the Sikorsky S-51 which, following a little redesign work, became the Dragonfly and entered service with the Royal Navy and RAF in 1953. The S-55 followed as the Whirlwind, and the S-58, re-engined with a gas turbine, became the Wessex. This line continues through to today, with the Sea King, a Sikorsky design that has been thoroughly redeveloped by Westland. Other projects have included the Westminster heavy-lift helicopter and a number of other helicopter and hovercraft designs following the acquisition of the rotary wing interests of the Fairey Bristol and Saunders Roe companies (these

The last of Westland's designs produced during the wartime period was the Wyvern.
The prototype is seen flying in 1946. (Aeroplane)

include the Rotodyne, Belvedere, Wasp and Scout). Joint ventures with other companies have resulted in the manufacture of the Bell Sioux, (with Agusta) and the Puma, Gazelle and Lynx, with Aerospatiale.

Today, aircraft production is still very much in evidence at Yeovil. The successors to the Westland Aircraft factory, Agusta Westland, produce the Sea King, Lynx, and Merlin, examples of which can often be seen on test and evaluation flights at the airfield.

13
YEOVILTON

2 miles east of Ilchester
ST 550234

In June 1940 RNAS Yeovilton was commissioned by the Royal Navy as HMS *Heron,* and to this day it is one of the Fleet Air Arm's major airfields. It is also the home of the Fleet Air Arm Museum. One of the first pilots to show an interest in the site was Harald Penrose, the Chief Test Pilot of the Westland Aircraft Company. In 1938 he was flying a Hawker Hector aircraft over the South Somerset plain, looking for a suitable site for an aerodrome, as his company needed to expand its facilities. He spotted the large fields in the Yeovilton area and made a good landing, which confirmed the area's suitability as an airfield. Although the Air Ministry approved Westland's subsequent proposal, the landowners, the Ecclesiastical Commission, refused to sell, and that was the end of things for the time being.

In the meantime the Royal Navy was also on the lookout for airfield sites. In 1937 there was a government decision to transfer control of the Fleet Air Arm (FAA) from the Air Ministry to the Admiralty, thus ending some 20 years of political wrangling. As part of the agreement some airfields had been transferred from one service to the other, but in order to create its own operational organization the Fleet Air Arm had to find additional ones. Yeovilton was one of the sites that had been identified as a potential base. Following a survey by Commander John Heath of the Admiralty Air Division, its acquisition was proposed, and so in July 1939 the Admiralty commandeered the land it needed – 417 acres of level farmland, just to the east of Ilchester – from the Ecclesiastical Commission. Work started shortly afterwards on the airfield, which was to be a flying training station. This was given added impetus with the outbreak of war in September.

Because the area formed part of the flood plain of the River Yeo, the builders experienced problems with drainage. Heavy rain in the autumn of 1939 accentuated the problem, and the locals jokingly asked visiting naval personnel whether they intended to build a seaplane base at Yeovilton! Nevertheless, throughout that winter, the construction gangs of the Ministry of Public Buildings and Works laboured away and by the spring of 1940 the layout of the new airfield had taken shape. A main runway, 3,645 feet long, had been constructed on a south-west/north-west axis, along with three subsidiary runways, each of 3,000 feet, in what was to become a typical naval flying training pattern. The first officer to command the emerging airfield was Commander Robert Poole, and he set up his headquarters in Rag Cottages, the only permanent buildings then within the airfield perimeter.

In May 1940 Yeovilton was still far from complete when it received its first units. These were 750, 751 and 752 squadrons, which together made up No. 1 Naval Observers' School. They had been moved when their previous base, Ford, in Sussex, had been heavily bombed with many casualties. The Blackburn Sharks and Hawker Ospreys of 750 Squadron, the Walruses of 751 Squadron, and the Proctors and Albacores of 752 Squadron were thus the first Fleet Air Arm aeroplanes to be seen in the area.

On 2 June the first members of the station's staff (or 'ship's company'), a detachment of ratings from RN Barracks, Devonport, arrived to provide airfield defence. However, they were to find only rudimentary living quarters at Yeovilton. There was no permanent accommodation, so shelter was erected in the form of bell tents and marquees, and the food was provided by field kitchens. However, on 18 June 1940, in the naval tradition, Yeovilton airfield was commissioned as a ship, HMS *Heron*, under the command of Captain H.S. Murray-Smith, who had previously served with the China Fleet. Under him, the first Commander Flying was Commander Jan Sears. He was an experienced naval pilot and took his duties seriously. Every morning at 0730 hours he would make the first flight of the day, a 'met' flight, to check the

The Albacores of 752 Squadron were some of the first aircraft to operate from Yeovilton. (Aeroplane)

local weather and determine the cloud base, in preparation for the day's flying programme. His personal aircraft was a Gloster Sea Gladiator, which was kept in tip-top condition by the air mechanics.

Gradually the essential operational buildings were erected, as well as accommodation for the various members of the station's personnel. Among the hangars to be built early on was one for Westland Aircraft. The company had come to an early agreement with the Navy to have facilities at the new station, probably as the result of Westland's earlier disappointment at not being able to build the airfield themselves. In October 1939 the company purchased land at the western end of the airfield on which to construct a factory. This was to be the base of the Westland Repair Organization, known as the company's Ilchester factory. Beside the main building was an apron which gave access across Pyle Lane (which ran down the western perimeter of the airfield) onto the airfield itself. The company was also given the use of two Bellman hangars on the airfield side of Pyle Lane for the breakdown and salvage of damaged aircraft. Most of the work at the new factory unit consisted of rebuilding RAF Spitfires which had been damaged in flying accidents, or, more often as the war progressed, as a result of enemy action.

The summer of 1940 saw a lot of aerial activity over southern England. Although most of the Luftwaffe's attentions were concentrated on the South East, they did range further to the west

Luftwaffe target photograph of Yeovilton taken during the summer of 1940. (Nigel J Clarke Publications)

on many occasions. RNAS Yeovilton and the Westland airfield at Yeovil were both on the Luftwaffe's target maps, and the first attack on Yeovilton came in the late afternoon of 5 July 1940, when an unidentified aircraft was seen over the station. It was soon known to be hostile when it dived and dropped several bombs on the field. The aircraft, which turned out to be a Junkers JU88, created four large craters, but no one was injured. A further attack by a lone JU88 occurred on 15 July. The weather that day was not very good, and RAF fighters were unable to find a formation of JU88s that were heading for the Westland works at Yeovil. One of the German pilots took advantage of the overcast conditions to peel off and make a separate attack on Yeovilton. His low-level attack surprised the station's staff, and he dropped several bombs before making off. This time more substantial damage was caused, for, as well as craters in the airfield and perimeter road, one end of the Westland hangar was hit along with several buildings nearby. Five people were injured, including two men who were camouflaging the hangar roof at the time.

The accommodation was still being completed at this time, and the main contingent of the base's new personnel arrived in August, together with a party of Wrens. Although they might have thought that they had been posted to a station in the middle of nowhere, the new arrivals were soon reminded that they were part of the war. On the afternoon of 14 August Luftwaffe units mounted attacks over various parts of southern England. Among their targets were RAF Colerne, RAF Middle Wallop and RNAS Yeovilton, and a large aerial battle developed over that area, as RAF fighters were brought in to intercept the raiders. Air raid warnings were sounded, and everyone took cover or manned anti-aircraft guns. Out of the melée, one of the German bombers emerged over Yeovilton, its pilot dropping several bombs before escaping unscathed. Once again, craters appeared on the airfield, this time on one of the runways and a hardstanding. Some fuel bowsers were also hit.

In August 1940 the first squadron to be formed at Yeovilton came into being. This was 794 Squadron, which was initially equipped with the obsolescent Blackburn Roc fighter and Fairey Swordfish torpedo bombers. These aircraft were specially modified, as the squadron's role was to tow targets for trainee fighter pilots to

Fairey Swordfish flew with 794 Squadron from Yeovilton. A preserved example of the Royal Naval Historic Aircraft Flight is shown near the control tower in 2003. (Author)

practise their aerial gunnery. The squadron later received a few Blackburn Skuas, Supermarine Spitfires, Boulton Paul Defiants, de Havilland Tiger Moths and Bristol Blenheims. Their customers started to arrive six weeks later, as, on 16 September, the first aircraft of 759 and 760 squadrons flew in on dispersal to escape enemy attacks on their former base at Eastleigh, near Southampton.

759 Squadron had been formed at Eastleigh in November 1939 and became the Fleet Fighter School. It had nine Skuas, five Rocs and four Sea Gladiators on strength. Shortly after the unit's arrival at Yeovilton, these were augmented by Fairey Fulmars, Miles Masters and Grumman Martlets. The latter, known in the USA as 'Wildcats', were among the first of many US types to fly with the Fleet Air Arm during the Second World War. The first to arrive were French Navy aircraft that had been diverted to the UK after the fall of France. Shortly after arriving at Yeovilton the squadron received another US type, the Brewster Buffalo, which equipped

Buffalo Mk I AS417 which flew with 759 Squadron from Yeovilton during 1940. (Aeroplane)

US Navy fighter squadrons, but which was to prove not particularly successful. 760 Squadron had also been formed at Eastleigh, on 1 April 1940, with four Skuas, two Rocs and a Sea Gladiator, and moved to Yeovilton as the Fighter Pool Squadron. It too received Masters shortly after its arrival at Yeovilton. The squadron's task was to act as a holding unit for newly qualified fighter pilots and to keep their competence levels high by providing regular flying opportunities until they were posted to squadrons. Together, the units were responsible for training qualified pilots to become fighter pilots in order to man the many new Fleet Air Arm front-line squadrons that were being formed. Most of the squadrons' aircraft were kept fully armed during this period, which later became popularly known as the Battle of Britain, in case they encountered any unfriendly aircraft.

Having completed their primary and advanced flying training, potential fighter pilots were posted to Yeovilton. After initial assessment and tuition in the two-seat Master, the students were then taught to fly operational types such as the Sea Gladiator, Skua and Sea Hurricane. They then moved on to study such subjects as formation flying, interception, tactics and air-fighting. Using an area of one of the runways marked up as a flight-deck, they also had to learn to land on an aircraft carrier. Before graduating, the student fighter pilots had to perfect their gunnery, using ground targets and the aerial sleeve targets towed by 794 Squadron. The fully-trained fighter pilot would then move on to 760 Squadron, where he would build up his hours and experience on operational aircraft before he was assessed as being ready to join a front-line squadron.

From August 1940 the Observer School (751, 750, and 752 Squadrons) moved away from Yeovilton. On 19 August 751 Squadron was moved with its Walruses to Arbroath to become part of No. 2 Observers' School. It had been decided to move 750 and 752 squadrons overseas, and so after training ceased at Yeovilton on 28 September the personnel of both squadrons prepared for the move. First they went to Lee-on-Solent, and then, in mid-October, the squadron personnel embarked for Piarzo Savannah, Trinidad, where they resumed training on 5 November and continued to train observers for the rest of the war.

While the Observer School's squadrons were on the move, a new, front-line unit was forming up at Yeovilton. This was 827 Squadron, a torpedo spotter reconnaissance squadron, which officially came into existence on 15 September 1940 with twelve Fairey Albacores on strength. After a period of working up at Yeovilton, the squadron moved on in November to Crail in Scotland, where it undertook anti-submarine patrols and convoy escorts under the control of RAF Coastal Command, before joining the aircraft carrier HMS *Victorious* and taking part in attacks on German naval forces in Norway the following summer.

Captain Eric 'Winkle' Brown, later a celebrated test pilot, was a Sub-Lieutenant when he flew from Yeovilton in the autumn of 1940. He has memories of an airfield consisting of three half-completed runways in a sea of mud. Having joined 794 Squadron, he was given his introduction to the Blackburn Roc. When taxiing out, he had to avoid builders' lorries and construction plant. He was just taking off for his first solo in the type when he felt a thump on the undercarriage. He completed his take-off, retracted his

201

undercarriage, and continued with the flight, but on returning to land he found that only one undercarriage leg would come down. He contacted air traffic control and was instructed to retract the undercarriage and belly land in the mud alongside the runway. It was later found that the undercarriage that wouldn't lock down had been damaged by a pile of rubble that had been left on the runway!

By the time of the Battle of Britain, Westland's Ilchester works had become a major centre for the repair of battle- and accident-damaged Spitfires. Its works had also been expanded to include the modification of Curtiss Mohawks and Tomahawks for the RAF. These aircraft had been built for the French Air Force, but were diverted to Britain following the collapse of France. This work included the fitting of British radio equipment and the replacement of metric cockpit instruments.

Interspersed with the RAF work were urgent contracts for some of Westland's own products, including the stripping down of Lysanders ready for crating and shipment overseas. Malta was one of the first destinations for these, and they were required so urgently that the aircraft were flown to Yeovilton and stripped down in the Pyle Lane salvage hangars. Lysanders also came to Yeovilton for a different, classified reason: to convert a number for covert operations in occupied Europe in order to transport undercover agents and their equipment. Special radio equipment was fitted along with a large long-range fuel tank under the fuselage between the undercarriage legs, and a ladder was fixed to the port side of the fuselage for quick and easy entry and exit by the passengers. The aircraft were painted matt black overall, and had patches of luminous paint applied to the ladder rungs and cockpit edge, so that they could be easily located in the dark.

Westland's Ilchester factory also worked in support of the RAF's Whirlwind squadrons. These units were often based in the South West, within reasonable range of Yeovilton. When Whirlwind pilots had problems, having had a mechanical malfunction or even having been shot up, they would often fly to Yeovilton for running repairs. The Westland technicians would have a look at the problem, and often fix it while the pilot waited.

The second front-line unit to appear at Yeovilton was 807 Squadron, which moved in from St Merryn on 9 December 1940.

A Lysander seen outside the Pyle Lane hangars after conversion to clandestine transport. (Aeroplane).

This was a fleet fighter squadron flying Fulmar Mk Is. A detachment of three of its aircraft were aboard HMS Pegasus for catapult operations while the remainder of the unit flew on continuation training from Yeovilton. The squadron moved to Prestwick on 4 February 1941.

Following the German defeat in the Battle of Britain, Hitler cancelled Operation Sealion, the invasion of Britain. However, Luftwaffe raids continued during the autumn of 1940 and into the following winter, moving from daylight to night-time attacks. Several local towns, such as Yeovil, were bombed as German raiders roamed the skies over Somerset. Air raid alarms were sounded at Yeovilton many times, but on only one occasion during this period did the Luftwaffe attack the airfield. This was on 12 May 1941, when a lone JU88 appeared early that morning. It flew

Martlets were operated by several Yeovilton units, including 748, 759 and 762 Squadrons. (Aeroplane)

across the airfield and dropped eight high explosive and eight incendiary bombs. Fortunately they exploded harmlessly on the grass areas of the airfield and no one was hurt. To distract enemy pilots away from Yeovilton, a decoy airfield was constructed at Knole, four miles to the west of the main airfield. Runways and roads were laid out there, with lighting added to increase the effect at night. The decoy was convincing to at least one Luftwaffe pilot, who dropped four large parachute mines on it in late 1941.

In the spring of 1941, 759 Squadron, which had been flying its students in Gladiators and Fulmars, received a dozen Hurricanes from the RAF. These aircraft had been well-used by their former owners, with worn out brakes and tired engines that leaked oil. However, to the pilots of 759 Squadron who were used to the Sea Gladiator, they were seen as a leap forward in technology. They had awesome power in comparison, were agile in the air, and their wide-track undercarriage absorbed many a bad landing.

As well as training, from 1941 Yeovilton's role expanded to become a host station for fleet fighter squadrons. The first of these, 804 Squadron, arrived in February 1941, and soon after its Martlets and Buffalos were replaced by Fulmar IIs and Sea Hurricanes. With its headquarters at Yeovilton, the unit sent detachments to other naval air stations or ships as required, including Belfast and North Front (Gibraltar), and the carrier HMS *Pegasus*.

A new squadron, No. 787, was formed at Yeovilton on 5th March 1941. Created from an element of 804 Squadron, its role was to be the Fleet Fighter Development Unit and with three Fulmars and three Sea Gladiators its task was to evolve the Fleet Air Arm's fighter tactics its staff also evaluated new fighter aircraft types and compared them with naval ones. This included examples of enemy aircraft when they became available. One of the first such to arrive at Yeovilton was a Fiat CR42. This Italian biplane fighter had been shot down during the Battle of Britain, but as it was not badly damaged it was repaired and put back into the air. The CR42 was flown against the Gladiator in dogfights over the airfield. Both aircraft were flown by experienced fighter pilots, but it was generally agreed that the Italian fighter had the edge. The CR42 also did well against the Fulmar, which was much heavier and less manoeuvrable. The unit also had the use of a captured Bf109. The German fighter had already shown itself to be stiff competition for the RAF's front-line fighters, the Spitfire and Hurricane, and it was therefore no surprise that the Bf109 totally outclassed the Fulmar and Martlet when they were flown against it. In June 1941 the prefix 'Naval' was added to the unit's title, as it had been decided to move it to Duxford to be co-located with the RAF's AFDU, in order to enable the joint development of fighter tactics across all British fighter squadrons.

During the spring and summer of 1941, 804 Squadron still sent detachments aboard carriers such as HMS *Eagle* and HMS *Argus*. In May 1941, however, the squadron's role changed to include that of providing aircraft to operate from Catapult-Armed Merchant (CAM) ships. This was to counter one of the main threats to the Atlantic Convoys, the Focke-Wulf FW200 Condor. These four-engined, long-range maritime reconnaissance aircraft were based on the French coast and could range far out into the Atlantic in search of Allied shipping. On finding their quarry, the Condors

Several Sea Hurricane squadrons formed at Yeovilton during 1941. Here a preserved example revisits the station in 2003. (Author)

would either attack the ships with their own guns and bombs or notify marauding U-boats of their presence. Condors posed such a threat to British convoys beyond the range of land-based fighters that drastic measures had to be taken by the British to protect their shipping. The first such measure was the CAM ship, from which Sea Hurricanes or Fulmars could be catapulted on the appearance of a Condor. Once launched, the fighter pilots could not return to their ship; they either had to find land or ditch in the path of the convoy and hope to be rescued. The value of the CAM ship fighter in frightening off attackers, if not actually intercepting them, was demonstrated by the squadron on many occasions. On 3 August 1941, for example, Lieutenant R.W.H. Everett RNVR of 804 Squadron catapulted off HMS *Maplin*, a converted naval escort, in a Sea Hurricane and shot down a FW200 that had been shadowing the convoy. At least two detachments were lost when their ships were sunk – the SS *Michael E*, (the first CAM ship to be deployed), on 2 June 1941, and HMS *Springbok* on 27 September 1941. In May

1942 responsibility for the CAM ship role was transferred to the RAF's Merchant Ship Fighter Unit at Speke, and 804 Squadron moved away from Yeovilton the following month, to St Merryn in Cornwall.

Two more squadrons had appeared at Yeovilton on 1 August 1941. One of these was another fleet fighter squadron, No. 801. This unit had been disbanded in May 1941 following operations in Norway. Re-formed at Yeovilton with twelve Sea Hurricanes, the unit worked up to operational standard and then sent out a series of detachments, for example, to Scapa Flow, to defend the naval base there. On 6 October 1941, 801 was moved to St Merryn, and the following May went to the Mediterranean aboard HMS *Eagle*. However, the *Eagle* was torpedoed and sank on 11 August 1942 and the squadron ceased to exist.

Also formed at Yeovilton on 1 August 1941 was No. 761 Squadron as the Advanced Training Squadron of the Fleet Fighter School. Equipped with Fulmars I and II, and a few Sea Hurricane Ibs, the squadron's pilots used Haldon, a satellite of Yeovilton in South Devon, for firing practice and also undertook deck-landing practice with HMS *Argus* in the Channel. *Argus* was a converted Italian liner that had been requisitioned during the First World War. After a brief period of operational use in 1940, the ship was allocated as a deck-launching training carrier. On 10 April 1943, 761 became No. 2 Naval Air Fighter School and moved to Henstridge to create more room at Yeovilton.

883 Squadron was formed at Yeovilton on 10 October 1941, as a fleet fighter squadron with six Sea Hurricane IBs. The squadron's pilots were trained in fighter defence duties and spent their time in rehearsing tactics, forming fighter screens, and practising quick reaction alerts. At the end of January 1942 the squadron moved to Fraserburgh for embarkation aboard a carrier. While waiting for a ship the squadron's pilots maintained their skills by flying air defence patrols under 14 Group, RAF Fighter Command. They eventually joined HMS *Avenger*, which in September accompanied Convoy PQ18 to Russia as part of the escort. During this operation 883's pilots, together with those of 802 Squadron, shot down five German aircraft and damaged 17 others. The ship later took part in the North African landings and on 15 November 1942 while returning to the UK from this operation, she was

torpedoed by U-155. The ship blew up and 883 Squadron ceased to exist.

885 Squadron had seen limited operations in the Mediterranean before being disbanded in May 1941. It was re-formed at Yeovilton on 1 December 1941 as a fleet fighter squadron with six Sea Hurricane IBs and was intended for the escort carrier HMS *Charger*. However, the ship, a converted US merchantman, was retained by the US Navy to provide deck-landing training facilities for Fleet Air Arm squadrons forming up in the USA. Instead, 885 joined HMS *Victorious* in June 1942. In August the ship sailed for the Mediterranean and the squadron provided air cover for the Malta convoys. It later took part in the North African landings.

By late 1941, twelve large Bellman hangars and a technical hangar had been constructed at Yeovilton, and, although many Nissen and Maycrete huts had been built for domestic accommodation, more always seemed to be needed owing to the expansion of the station. Hangars were constructed at new dispersals established around the airfield on requisitioned land at Manor Farm, Specklington Farm, Bridgehampton and Podimore. However, these sites were occupied almost as soon as they were completed. Due to the pressure on space, a search for suitable sites for satellite airfields was made, and when the first of these, Henstridge and Charlton Horethorne, were opened in early 1942, the congestion at Yeovilton was eased by the transfer of some of the training units to the new airfields.

The importance of radar was demonstrated during the Battle of Britain when German raiders were detected in time for British fighters to be guided into position to intercept them. Although radar equipment had been in use by the Royal Navy since the early war years, it was not in widespread use in the fleet. During naval fighter operations, the pilots were briefed before take-off, but during their missions radio silence was kept in order to preserve security. However, during 1941 it was decided that naval pilots should benefit from the use of radar guidance, and towards the end of that year the Fighter Direction School, known as D-School, was set up at Yeovilton. Some of the first items of equipment used to train Air Direction Radar (ADR) operators were modified 'stop me and buy one' ice cream tricycles, which were pedalled by ratings and Wrens round a quiet corner of the airfield. They were in radio

Some of the 'ice cream tricycles' of the Fighter Direction School seen at Yeovilton during 1942. (Aeroplane)

contact with fighter controllers, who would direct 'fighter' tricycles in to intercept a 'bomber' tricycle. This was very rudimentary, but it did the trick. When ADR officers were posted to the fleet, the effectiveness of naval fighter interceptions increased considerably.

Lodged in the control tower, the school came to need more space and was moved to Speckington Manor on the north-eastern edge of the airfield in mid-1942, where the rooms were modified to simulate warship operations rooms. From 1942 work with actual aircraft was introduced into the training syllabus, although initial training on tricycles was kept. The students worked with the Airspeed Oxford and Fairey Fulmers of 790 Squadron, which had been re-formed at the satellite airfield at Charlton Horethorne. After an intensive three months' course, the trained ADR officers were posted to aircraft carriers, air defence cruisers, and operational bases around the world. Former ADR officers who trained at Yeovilton include an Attorney General, Sir Michael

Havers, and two distinguished actors, Michael Hordern and Kenneth More.

More squadron activity took place at Yeovilton in early 1942. 802 Squadron had been a Martlet squadron serving aboard HMS *Audacity* escorting Gibraltar convoys, when the ship was sunk by U-741 on 21 December 1941 and the squadron went down with it. However, the unit was re-formed as a fleet fighter squadron at Yeovilton on 1 February 1942 with six Sea Hurricane IBs. Having worked up to operational standard, the squadron embarked aboard HMS *Avenger* in September 1942. It provided air cover for the ships escorting convoy PQ18 to Russia and shared the aerial victories with 883 Squadron. It also shared its fate, eventually going down with HMS *Avenger* in November 1942, west of Gibraltar.

No. 884, a fleet fighter squadron with Fulmars, arrived from St Merryn on 7 February 1942 for a six-week stay. It left for air defence duties in Scotland on 22 March, under 14 Group, RAF, based at Turnhouse. The unit embarked aboard HMS *Victorious* in July to join the Malta convoys.

In March 1942, 762 Squadron formed at Yeovilton as an advanced flying training school, with Fulmars. It moved to St Merryn in mid-April, where it received Martlets and Masters, returning to Yeovilton on 8 September, when Sea Hurricanes were added to its inventory. The squadron then undertook conversion and continuation training. It was eventually absorbed into 761 Squadron at Henstridge on 9 June the following year.

887 Squadron, another fleet fighter squadron, appeared at Yeovilton on 1 June 1942, having been formed at Lee-on-Solent a month earlier with Fulmar IIs. On 10 July it moved to Charlton Horethorne, and on the 25th to St Merryn. The squadron was later earmarked for escort carriers, and re-equipped with Seafires, it took part in the Malta convoys and in the Salerno landings.

807 Squadron returned to Yeovilton during the summer of 1942. It had taken part in the Malta convoys the previous year, and four of its aircraft had survived the sinking of its carrier, HMS *Ark Royal*, on 13 November 1941 by flying to Gibraltar. Having taken part in further Malta convoys during the spring and early summer of 1942, the squadron returned to Yeovilton on 12 July to become the first to receive Seafires, specifically, the Seafire Mk IB. It trained with these while re-equipping with twelve of the more advanced IICs. At the

Fulmars flew with several squadrons from Yeovilton. This one is seen practising a dummy deck landing. (Aeroplane)

end of August 1942, the squadron joined HMS *Furious*, via Machrishanish in Scotland, and returned to the Mediterranean. No. 807 subsequently took part in the North African landings, during which its pilots shot down two Vichy-French fighters and damaged two others as well as two more on the ground.

Meanwhile the work of the training units at Yeovilton continued, with the accent on the production of new fighter pilots. 759 Squadron had been steadily increasing in size to reflect the requirements placed upon it. In April 1943 the squadron had become the advanced flying school component of No. 1 Naval Air Fighter School and by May it had a sizeable complement of aircraft, comprising 66 Sea Hurricanes, eight Spitfires, 24 Fulmars, and 15 Martlets. Also by this time, 794 Squadron, that had been providing air target towing facilities for the Yeovilton squadrons, had grown in size and had 16 Sea Hurricanes, four Masters, four Defiants and eight Martinets on strength. In July 1943 it was decided to move air firing training to Angle. Accordingly, 794 Squadron left Yeovilton on 1 July 1943, and with it went a detachment of 759 Squadron. Its primary role remained that of acting as a target towing and air firing training unit for the Fighter School at Yeovilton. Together with the 759 Squadron detachment, the squadron was re-titled the Naval Air Firing Unit.

Another unit came into being at Yeovilton when, on 24 May 1943, 736 Squadron was formed as the School of Air Combat. This move came about following the decision by the Fleet Air Arm to take on the role themselves of teaching the latest techniques of air combat to experienced naval fighter leaders. Hitherto this had been done by the RAF Fighter Leaders School at Charmy Down in Gloucestershire. Equipped with Seafires, the school got up and running under its CO Lieutenant Commander Jimmy Gardner. One of the Fleet Air Arm's most experienced fighter pilots, Gardner had flown with Douglas Bader's 242 Squadron during the Battle of Britain. The school was soon hard at work, and when the value of its role was realized, it was decided to combine it with the School of Naval Air Warfare as the Fighter Combat School. This, however, meant a move, and on 12 September the squadron headed off to its new base at St Merryn.

A couple of days before 736's departure, a new squadron came into being at Yeovilton: a RN Volunteer Reserve Squadron, No. 1770, which was the first of several two-seater fighter squadrons formed to fly the Fairey Firefly Mk I. Equipped with a dozen aircraft, the squadron spent the next few months getting to know the new machines and working up to operational status. In May 1944 the squadron joined HMS *Indefatigable* and took part in operations against the German battleship *Tirpitz* in Tromso Fjord, Norway. Their particular task was to attack defensive gun positions and auxiliary vessels in the fjord. The squadron took part in further operations against the *Tirpitz* in August and later sailed with the *Indefatigable* to the Far East for operations against the Japanese.

Being in rural Somerset in 1943, the personnel of Yeovilton were not often directly involved in hostilities. There were occasional alarms when evening intruders were detected, but they were rarely actually seen. Towards the end of the year, however, graphic reminders of the air war over Europe started to appear at Yeovilton in the form of US bombers returning from the Continent. As the daylight air offensive by the USAAF built up, so did the casualties, indicating the strength of the German defences. One of the first arrivals at Yeovilton was Boeing B-17 Fortress *Mispah* of the 91st

Seafire Mk IB of 736 Squadron, part of No 1 Naval Air Fighter School, seen at Yeovilton in September 1943. (Aeroplane)

Bombardment Group, based at Bassingbourn, Cambridgeshire. The aircraft had been involved in a mid-air collision during a raid on the U-boat pens at St Nazaire, which put both starboard engines out of action. Although none of the crew was injured in the collision, they were extremely lucky to be able to make it back to Yeovilton. Other incoming B-17s and B-24 Liberators did not have quite so fortunate a story; aboard aircraft that had been hit by flak or fighter shells there were often wounded or dead crewmen. Once the crew had been attended to, the aircraft would be towed to dispersals to await the attention of USAAF mobile working parties. They would either repair the aircraft to enable them to return to base by air or disassemble them for transport by road.

On 11 October 1943 B Flight of 748 Squadron had moved to Yeovilton from St Merryn. Also known as No. 10 Naval Operational Training Unit (OTU), the squadron's role was to provide operational and refresher training on front-line fighters and it was therefore equipped with Hurricanes, Sea Hurricanes, Martlets, Spitfires and Seafires. When the main squadron moved from St Merryn to Henstridge in February 1944, B Flight rejoined it, but returned to Yeovilton on 9 March 1944 when the whole squadron transferred. At Yeovilton 748 Squadron received Corsairs and Hellcats, and in June a few Fireflys arrived. The squadron moved to Dale on 1 October 1944. Another Firefly squadron to form at Yeovilton was No. 1771, another RNVR unit, on 1 February 1944. With a dozen Firefly Mk Is, it followed the pattern of conversion training and work-up before moving to Burscough for embarkation aboard HMS *Implacable* in September 1944. It then took part in operations in Norway, flying reconnaissance missions over Tromso, including the *Tirpitz's* anchorage, and flying strikes against German shipping in the area. The following spring the ship, with its squadrons, set sail to join the British Pacific Fleet.

On 15th March 1944, 762 Squadron reappeared at Yeovilton. It had been re-formed from part of 798 Squadron, based at Lee on Solent. The unit had been running advanced conversion courses, with an assortment of aircraft. 762 Squadron was formed to concentrate on twin-engine type conversions, and so brought with it to Yeovilton a number of Bristol Beauforts, Blenheims and Beaufighters, as well as Airspeed Oxfords. On 31 March 1944 the squadron moved to Dale.

In stark contrast to many of the other airfields in the region which were involved to a greater or lesser degree with preparations for the invasion of Europe, Yeovilton had a quiet summer in 1944 apart from the daily routine of flying training. This was because Yeovilton's training role was seen as a vitally important one for the Fleet Air Arm, and one that was not to be curtailed if at all possible. That was not to say, of course, that the station's flying was not to be interrupted by the occasional emergency landing by troop-carrying gliders, or tugs on training exercises in the area.

One of the last wartime arrivals at Yeovilton, on 22 September 1944, was 835 Squadron, which made a brief stay. The unit had formed as a torpedo bomber reconnaissance squadron at Palisadoes in Jamaica on 15 February 1942, with four Swordfish Mk Is. The squadron later formed a fighter flight of six Sea Hurricanes and by 1944 it was aboard HMS *Nairana*, an escort carrier on the Atlantic convoys. 835 Squadron encountered several enemy aircraft, and during May and June it claimed two Junkers JU290 long-range bombers in mid-Atlantic. The squadron received the later mark of Swordfish, the Mk III, in July, and it was on returning from an Atlantic convoy in September that the unit arrived at Yeovilton to exchange the Sea Hurricanes for the later mark of Martlet (then known as the Wildcat), the Wildcat Mk VI. When 835 Squadron returned to sea on 4 October, HMS *Nairana* had been switched to the Russian convoys, and the squadron spent the winter of 1944-45 flying the route to Murmansk and back. One of the author's uncles, Harold Carman, a Cornishman, served as a ground engineer with 835 Squadron aboard HMS *Nairana*. He remembered the harsh and trying conditions of the Russian convoys, and did not envy the aircrews who had to fly operations in all weathers in the open cockpit Swordfish aircraft. The squadron's aircraft found and attacked two U-boats during this time, and shot down four enemy aircraft.

759 Squadron carried on with its training role during this time, and in the autumn of 1944 had a few Spitfires and Seafires on strength, together with Wildcats. Its Masters were being gradually

Vought Corsairs were operated by 748 and 759 Squadrons from Yeovilton. (Aeroplane)

replaced by Harvards, and, as Corsairs became available in larger numbers, they too were issued to the squadron. By November 1944 the unit had largely re-equipped with the type. The large cranked-wing fighters were a familiar sight in the Yeovilton circuit in early 1945, as by then over 150 of them were flying from the station. A Flight of 759 Squadron provided basic type conversions onto the Seafire or Corsair, usually straight from the North American Harvard trainer. The leap in performance between the two types was impressive (from the 550 hp Harvard to the 2,000 hp Corsair), but unfortunately this caused problems for many pupil pilots and the accident rate was high. Once qualified on type, the pilots moved on to C Flight for combat instruction and air-to-air firing, and then on to D flight to practise dummy deck-landings. The latter stage was particularly important, as the Corsair was a notoriously difficult aircraft to fly, and many accidents occurred during the landing phase, owing to the high power of the aircraft and the fact that its large propeller was kept off the ground by its cranked wing and long undercarriage, which made it difficult to judge the aircraft's height at the critical touch-down stage of landing.

For most of 1945, 759 Squadron was the only squadron to operate at Yeovilton, converting pilots onto Seafires, Corsairs, and later Wildcats. VE Day was a justified cause for a massive celebration at the airfield. A large bonfire was made of blackout boards and curtains, and every pyrotechnic device that could be laid hands on was fired into the night sky over the station. A more sobering but no less welcome effect of the war's end arrived at Yeovilton shortly after VE Day in the form of repatriated Prisoners of War, flown in by Dakotas of the RAF. However, as the war with the Japanese was still in full swing, 759 Squadron's job carried on, as did the need for pilots to reinforce the Far East Fleet.

Several Yeovilton-formed squadrons and many Yeovilton pilots fought on in the Far East over the following months. One of the most distinguished of these was Lieutenant Robert Hampton Gray, a Canadian who had graduated from Yeovilton in 1941. By August 1945 he had become senior pilot of 841 Squadron and had already been awarded the DSC for his bravery earlier in the year, flying Corsairs from HMS *Formidable* off the coast of Japan. On 9 August 1945, the day on which the second atom bomb was dropped, he was briefed to lead a flight of Corsairs on a sweep over the southern Japanese home islands to check on the disposition of enemy forces along the coastline. As the fighters passed over the small inlet of Onagawa Wan, one of the pilots spotted a small flotilla of ships and Gray ordered the flight to dive and investigate. The Japanese started firing and soon a heavy flak barrage was being directed on the Corsairs. Gray decided to go for one of the escort ships, the *Amakusa*, but as he dived towards it his Corsair was hit by a flak shell and caught fire. Gray pressed home his attack and scored a hit with his bomb on the superstructure of the ship. As the *Amakusa* started to burn, Gray's blazing Corsair plunged into the bay and was never seen again. Lieutenant Robert Hampton Gray DSC RNVR was awarded the Victoria Cross for his actions that day, only the second Victoria Cross awarded to an Allied fighter pilot during the Second World War.

Following VJ Day, the run-down of Britain's armed forces started, and Yeovilton became one of the main demobilization centres for the Royal Navy. When the airfield was closed for flying in September 1945, 759 Squadron was moved to Zeals, but it was decided to retain Yeovilton for the time being and to give the airfield's runways and taxiways a well-needed refurbishment. There were few pieces of mechanical plant available, but there was plenty of spare labour from the Demob Centre, as at any one time there were hundreds of men awaiting their honourable discharge from the Royal Navy or Royal Navy Volunteer Reserve. Officers were given crash courses in runway construction, and, under the supervision of a couple of civilian engineers, they organized the digging up of thousands of feet of runway. New foundations were then laid and filled in, ready for civilian contractors to top off with the final layer of tarmac.

When 759 Squadron returned to Yeovilton with the reopening of the airfield in January 1946, it had a larger complement, as it had absorbed 761 Squadron at Henstridge. With the end of the war, most of the US aeroplanes that had been supplied under lend-lease had been returned. A few Corsairs and Hellcats had been retained with US permission, but the squadron was now equipped mostly with Seafires of the later, more advanced, Griffon-engined type. However, 759's post-war existence at Yeovilton was not to last long, for on 5 February 1946, it was absorbed into 794 Squadron, the School of Air Firing, which had re-formed at St. Merryn.

Sea King commando helicopters fly from Yeovilton today, as seen during the annual flying display in 2005. (Author)

700 Squadron, the Maintenance Test Pilots' School, arrived from Middle Wallop in April 1946. The school ran a course of ten weeks, during which students were taught to test-fly the basic types of aircraft then in service (i.e. the Grumman Avenger, Hellcat and Wildcat, the Fairey Barracuda and Firefly, Blackburn Firebrand, and Supermarine Seafire). The squadron disbanded at Yeovilton on 30 September 1949.

Disembarked Firefly and Sea Fury squadrons were accommodated at Yeovilton during 1948–49, and 767 Squadron transferred from Milltown on 8 September 1948 with its Seafires and Fireflies to give deck-landing control officer training, nicknamed the 'clockwork mouse' squadron because of the continual circuits and landings of its aircraft, 767 Squadron stayed until 1952.

This trickle of squadrons reflected the uncertainty of Yeovilton's status, but a decision was made in 1952 that was to secure its future. This was that Yeovilton was to become the shore base for the Fleet's all-weather fighters. Paradoxically, the station was then closed, but an extensive rebuilding programme was undertaken by Taylor Woodrow Ltd, including the lengthening of two runways. Yeovilton became an all-jet air station in 1956, and over the following 40 years or so it has been the Fleet Air Arm's main jet fighter base.

Although Westland had to hand back the two Bellman salvage hangars at the war's end, the company's work on Spitfire refurbishment continued. A series of contracts kept the Ilchester factory going for many years, including the modification of jet fighters and the refurbishment of helicopters. The factory was eventually sold to the Ministry of Defence in 1985 and refurbished to house Commando helicopters.

Still under Fleet Air Arm control, Yeovilton today is one of the busiest military airfields in the UK and is amongst the largest in Europe, normally housing nine squadrons and up to 150 aircraft of various types. Even though the Sea Harrier squadrons are no more, the continued need for naval helicopters to operate from Yeovilton will hopefully continue for some time yet.

14
CIVILIANS AT WAR

To say that the international situation was a little strained during the summer of 1939 is an understatement. The outbreak of hostilities had been expected during the autumn of 1938, when the Munich crisis that September brought Germany to the brink of war. Things then settled down, but, although everyone hoped for a lasting peace, most people feared the worst. The publication and issue to all households of four Public Information Leaflets in July 1939 did not help matters. Entitled 'Some things you should know if war should come', 'Your gas mask', 'Your food in wartime', and 'Evacuation, when and how', the pamphlets were helpfully endorsed with the words 'This does not mean that war is expected now'.

During the Munich Crisis an Air Raid Precautions Act was invoked, which resulted in the formation of a Civil Defence Corps and the recruitment of volunteers such as auxiliary firemen, ambulance drivers, and air raid wardens. Respirators (or gas masks, as they were more popularly known) were issued to the civilian population as well as the armed forces, to be carried at all times should war come.

In March 1939 Germany invaded Czechoslovakia, forcing Neville Chamberlain, the British Prime Minister, to abandon his policy of appeasement towards Germany. He pledged that Britain would come to the aid of Poland if it too was attacked by Germany.

Conscription was then started in Britain, and the civil defence volunteers started training in earnest. Anderson air-raid shelters

Photograph of pre-war air raid precautions exercise, in June 1939, taken by the author's father. (Geoff Berryman)

had been put into production and were made available to families throughout Britain. Public air-raid shelters were built in towns, and, to protect public buildings from blast damage, sandbags were piled against their walls.

The Air Raid Precautions (ARP) organisation's main function was to protect the public, to warn them of impending air raids, and then to co-ordinate any rescue or emergency measures that were required. Somerset was divided into nine areas for civil defence purposes (Clevedon, Bathavon, Weston-super-Mare, Bridgwater, Wells, Yeovil, Taunton, Minehead and the City of Bath), co-ordinated by the Somerset County Civil Defence control room in the basement of County Hall, Taunton. Wardens were appointed for each of the areas, to patrol and ensure that the blackout regulations were being observed. Should an air raid warning be received, it would be issued to the areas affected, so that the alarms could be sounded and the population shepherded to the air-raid

Preserved Austin fire tender of the National Fire Service. (Author)

shelters. The ARP wardens worked with the local police, assisted by Police War Reserves and the Special Constabulary, and also the Auxiliary Fire Service, that had been formed to assist the county fire brigade. Other civil defence volunteers included rescue parties (there were 39 in Somerset, each consisting of 28 personnel), decontamination squads (26 in Somerset, of a similar size), and first aid parties (Somerset had 107, each of 20 personnel, supported by 108 ambulances, each with a crew of two).

As the international crisis worsened, on 22 August 1939 the British Government reaffirmed its pledge to Poland. Two days later the shocking news was received that Germany and the USSR had signed a non-aggression pact. Later that day the Emergency Powers (Defence) Act was passed in Parliament, which gave the authorities wide-ranging powers contained in over 100 regulations, covering all aspects of the defence of the realm. Houses could, for example, be entered and searched without reason or warning, property or land could be requisitioned for war use, people could be forcibly evacuated from designated areas, the ports and railways were to be taken over by the government, and bus and train services could be cut back. Reservists were called up that same day, and on the 25th a Treaty of Alliance was signed with Poland. On 31 August it was announced that the mass evacuation of children from London would start. The following morning tens of thousands of children with name tags, respirators, and a few precious possessions, assembled at bus and railway stations ready to be moved into the countryside. Many thousands were to arrive in the towns and villages of Somerset. Indeed, by 1 August 1940 the evacuees that had arrived in the county numbered 24,776 unaccompanied children, 970 accompanied children, 472 mothers, 1,340 teachers, and 269 others, a total of 27,527. By January 1941 this total had increased to 62,874.

A lorry drove into the courtyard of the disused prison at Shepton Mallet on 22 August 1939, and its crates were unloaded. More vehicles followed on a daily basis over the next few months. Eventually about 10,000 crates containing some of the nation's most historic documents that had been evacuated from the Public Record Office in London filled the prison's cells. These included Domesday Book and original records from the 12th to the 14th centuries. Priceless exhibits from the Victoria and Albert Museum were later taken to Montacute House near Yeovil for safe-keeping.

The inevitable occurred, and German tanks rolled into Poland on 1 September 1939. Britain issued an ultimatum for Germany to withdraw from Poland, but, as 'no such undertaking had been received' by 11 am on 3 September, Neville Chamberlain announced in a radio broadcast to the nation that Britain was at war with Germany. The forces were mobilized, and shortly afterwards the British Expeditionary Force was sent to France along with RAF squadrons of the Advanced Air Striking Force to support it. There, however, they stayed, and the 'Phoney War' followed, as the expected German air raids did not materialize, nor did waves of German tanks and troops appear at the French border. The French were confidently sitting within and behind their much vaunted Maginot Line, backed up by the BEF, and they continued to wait.

In Britain there was a sigh of relief, at least at government level, as defensive preparations were needed to meet the German offensive, which was bound to come eventually. Among such measures was the installation of local defence positions, remnants of which are still quite common today in the form of pillboxes. They appear to be randomly placed in fields and alongside roads, but in fact they were carefully positioned in accordance with a master plan, which had been developed by General Sir Edmund Ironside, Commander-in-Chief Home Forces. The plan called for defence in depth: lines of coastal defences, backed up by layers of further defensive installations inland. London and the Midlands were to be protected by a line of defences known as the GHQ line, with a series of Command, Corps, and Divisional stop-lines between it and the coast. The stop lines were reinforced by a series of local lines of defence that incorporated roads, railway embankments, rivers and canals. Pillboxes and road blocks within these lines were to be manned by locally-based soldiers or Home Guard defenders to prevent enemy troops from making a breakthrough into the country's interior. There were also 'point defences' built around important road or rail junctions, bridges, or other natural choke-points to prevent the movement of troops or vehicles through it. The lines used natural topography to produce a continuous anti-tank obstacle, with pillboxes overlooking strategic points and providing cover for each other. Columns of vehicle-mounted troops would be brought up to reinforce any threatened areas, and, should the enemy break through, he would be harried by the Home Guard Auxiliary Units.

Work on these defences started towards the end of June 1940, shortly after the plans had been approved by the government. Under the co-ordination of the Fortifications and Works Branch of the Royal Engineers, hundreds of local authorities and civilian contractors across the country began constructing thousands of pillboxes, anti-tank obstacles, and fire-positions. Pillboxes were of several types in standard designs, although local variations were allowed to suit particular locations, for example, to simulate beach-huts or ice-cream booths at the seaside, or as railway line-side sheds or farm outhouses further inland. Anti-tank obstacles included concrete 'dragon's teeth' or bespoke ones made out of steel rails. Construction teams worked long shifts during the summer of 1940 to prepare the defences. The final results were impressive and on a scale that was on a par with the ongoing

Surviving two-storey pillbox alongside a railway bridge near Bridgwater. (Author)

project to build hundreds of airfields for the RAF and Fleet Air Arm.

In Somerset part of the GHQ stop line (codename Green) went from Highbridge on the coast to Freshford, south of Bath, then across the county border to Stroud, and on to a point six miles south-west of Gloucester. It covered a linear distance of 91 miles, and consisted of 319 pillboxes with 20 miles of anti-tank ditches. The Taunton stop line also crossed Somerset, from the estuary of the River Parrett south of Highbridge to Seaton at the mouth of the river Axe on the English Channel coast, and consisted of 355 pillboxes. In addition the GHQ stop-line 'Yellow' ran from the confluence of the rivers Avon and Frome and crossed the county boundary into Wiltshire. It had 46 pillboxes in Somerset. Strong points were also constructed along the Somerset coast, totalling 233 pillboxes, and another 112 were incorporated into airfield defences. A number of smaller pillboxes were positioned as part of road blocks and to cover road junctions in towns. In total there were

Remains of a pillbox near Watchet, after having fallen victim to cliff erosion in 2005. (Author)

probably over a thousand pillboxes in Somerset alone. Local variants in pillbox designs and finishes included a pebble-facing on Porlock beach pillboxes (to blend in with the beach), fake newspaper kiosks and beach cafés on Minehead and Blue Anchor promenades, cowsheds and poultry houses on Sedgemoor, a water tower on the GWR line at Ilton, and a signal box on the railway line at Creech.

The coastal defences were supplemented by the rearming of old fortifications that had been built along the Bristol Channel during Victorian times, including batteries at Portishead, Avonmouth, Brean Down, and on the islands of Steep Holm and Flat Holm in mid-channel. The fort at Brean Down for example was equipped with two ex-naval 6-inch Mk VII CP coastal guns, and four of these guns were installed on Steep Holm in April 1942. Lewis guns were also provided for anti-aircraft defence at both locations.

On 10 May 1940 Winston Churchill became Prime Minister at the head of a coalition government. One of the first actions of the new government was to broadcast an appeal for men between the ages of 17 and 65 to volunteer their services in defence of the country against invasion. Volunteers would not be paid, but would be issued with weapons and uniforms. It was hoped that a force of 150,000 men might be raised, but within two weeks over 400,000 had volunteered, and this figure increased to one million a month later. Known at first as the Local Defence Volunteers, the men were issued with armbands with the initials LDV printed on them (which led to their being jokingly referred to as the 'Look, Duck and Vanish brigade'). In the absence of the promised weapons, they armed themselves with pitchforks and shotguns. On 15 June 1940 administration of the LDVs was taken on by the Territorial Army Association, and they were organized into battalions on a geographical basis. A southern area of command was formed, and Somerset became a LDV Zone, with its headquarters at Taunton. Uniforms were issued in July, and later that month the weapons arrived, in the form of one million Springfield rifles and 1,000 field guns with ammunition, presented by the government and people of the USA.

Shortly afterwards the LDV were retitled the Home Guard, and with their weapons and uniforms they looked and felt like a fighting force. They were not short of expertise, as many of those in the Home Guard ranks were old soldiers from the First World War. They soon became musketry and bombing instructors. Their tuition was supplemented by instructors from the Somerset Light Infantry, to whom Home Guard units in the county were affiliated for training. By October 1940 the Somerset Home Guard consisted of 13 battalions, each of between 2,000 and 3,000 men. The county was divided in two, with seven battalions in the North Group, and six in the South Group, the dividing line being from Burnham-on-Sea to Street, and then to Kilmington on the Wiltshire border. Better uniforms and equipment soon followed, and eventually staff cars and trucks were supplied. Some units used horses, such as the First Somerset (Minehead) Battalion, which could cover extensive stretches of Exmoor by using mounted patrols.

Home Guard Auxiliary Units were located in some parts of the county. Formed in secret, these units consisted of volunteers who, if the Germans did successfully invade Britain, were prepared to go into hiding and act as resistance squads to operate behind enemy lines, attacking arms dumps, lines of communication, airfields, and military headquarters. They usually operated in teams of four from dugouts concealed in the countryside, where they also secreted caches of arms and explosives. They were sworn to the strictest secrecy, and even today no one knows just how many Auxiliary Units were actually formed, and where many of their hideouts or caches of weapons were! By mid-1942 the Home Guard numbered 1.2 million troops. They developed into a well-trained force that was used as a reserve army, freeing up regular units for other military duties until they were stood down in December 1944.

Sacrifices had to be made by the British population as the war went on. Due to the decrease in food and supplies arriving in British ports following U-boat attacks on Merchant shipping, rationing increased and soon covered most food items. Every member of the civilian population was issued with a ration book to show and monitor their weekly food allowances, and each shop-keeper was allowed to have only a specified number of registered customers. His books were regularly audited to ensure that his supplies balanced with his sales to those customers, and there were severe penalties for irregularities. Despite this, however, there was a thriving black market and almost anything could be obtained if you knew who to ask and were prepared to pay the going rate!

Everyone was expected to supplement their rations by growing food in their gardens. Under the 'Dig for Victory' campaign people were encouraged to turn their lawns and flower beds into vegetable patches and to use any available land for allotments. The scheme was also extended to army camps and RAF stations, some of which became self-sufficient for many crops. Clothing was rationed and people had to make do and mend. 'Save' became another watchword, and everyone was encouraged to support campaigns for saving metal, saucepans, rags, bones, rubber and paper. During 1941 railings were cut down for scrap, and towns lost their ornamental cannon. The First World War tanks that had been presented to most towns as war memorials were unceremoniously towed away to be scrapped for the war effort.

As a concession to the clothing ration, the Church of England graciously relaxed its rule requiring women to wear hats in church in November 1941. A year later soap rationing was introduced (one tablet per person per month!), and bath water was restricted to a depth of five inches. Because of food rationing, there were official concerns about the nation's health, and housewives were bombarded with pamphlets providing nutritional information, such as 'Food Facts' and 'Food Hints'. In an effort to ensure that people should be able to have at least one nourishing cooked meal a day, community food centres, known as British Restaurants, were set up in most towns and cities. There, for fourpence a good breakfast could be had, and lunch for one shilling. By 1943 the restaurants had become an established part of urban life, with over 2,000 then in operation. In villages there was the Rural Pie Scheme, set up in 1942 by the Women's Voluntary Service, which provided over a million pies and snacks per week to some 5,000 villages scattered throughout the country.

The war must have seemed all-encompassing to the civilian population between the years of 1939 and 1945. It was a period of total war, and everyone in Britain was involved. Women volunteered to do their bit, and many joined the Women's Voluntary Service (WVS), an organization which had been formed in 1938 to encourage women into Civil Defence. The WVS made a vital contribution to the home front, and, often operating under difficult conditions, the 'Women in Green', as they were known from their uniforms, performed a variety of tasks. These included caring for the victims of air raids, running rest and reception centres for war workers and service personnel, organizing the collection of salvage, and operating canteens. Other female war workers included those of the Women's Land Army (WLA). Formed in June 1939, the strength of the WLA had risen to 17,000 by the outbreak of war. Attracted to the outdoor life, many found the days to be hard, long and exhausting, but those who stuck it out won the respect of a sceptical farming community. At its peak the Land Army was 87,000 strong, and provided a vital resource for the farming industry, which made a valuable contribution to the nation's survival.

Although many women were already involved in the war effort, at the end of 1942 the government introduced conscription for women. Britain was the only combatant nation to introduce this measure during the Second World War; even Germany never felt

WVS volunteers outside their HQ in Bath, c1941. (Bath Blitz Memorial Project)

the need to do it. All unmarried women between the ages of 20 and 30 were called up and given the choice of joining one of the three women's services, the Civil Defence or working in Industry. Many women went to work for the first time in this way. Coupled to this measure was the Essential Work Order, that transferred workers from what were regarded as non-essential jobs into those directly related to the war effort. Coming from all walks of life, from milkmen and salesmen to waitresses and librarians, people were uprooted from their homes, friends and families to be sent off to unfamiliar parts of the country where they would live in lodgings and work in strange factories. Nonetheless, this workforce, of whom over half were women, produced supplies and equipment that were essential for the armed forces and without which ultimate victory would not have been possible.

Essential war production in Somerset was centred on the aircraft industry, with the Westland Aircraft Company at Yeovil and Ilchester and the Bristol Aeroplane Company at Old Mixon and

230

Hutton, near Weston-super-Mare. There was also Avimo Ltd, which made optical gunsights in Taunton, and other sub-contractors to the aircraft manufacturers, such as Butler and Tanner of Frome, who machined components for Bristol aero engines. Other manufacturers producing essential materials for the war effort in the county included Stothert and Pitt, who made cranes, tank turret mountings and midget submarines at their works in Bath, Denning's Foundry in Chard, which made tank wheels, and a number of companies in Bridgwater, such as Electro-Dynamic Construction, which made electric motors for tanks and aircraft, the Light Buoyant Company, which constructed landing craft, Trojan Ltd, which produced shell cases, and British Cellophane, which made packaging film for such items as cigarettes, rations, blood plasma and ammunition.

Another, more unlikely, Somerset industry that contributed to the war effort was the withy weaving trade. From withies (osier stems) grown on the Somerset Levels, wicker seats were made for aeroplanes during the First World War, as well as wicker baskets for carrier pigeons. The latter were also produced for the armed forces during the Second World War, along with much larger baskets which were produced in their thousands for the delivery of supplies by parachute and were essential items for Britain's airborne forces.

Somerset was chosen as the location for three defence-related government departments in 1939 as war was looming. The first of these was the Hydrographic Supplies Department, which produced charts for the Royal Navy. When it was decided to move the department out of the London area, Taunton was selected. A new building was erected to house its printing presses, and production started at the new site in 1941, where it continues today. On the outbreak of war the Admiralty evacuated several of its departments from the London area and moved them to Bath, taking over a number of buildings there, including the Pump Room, Pulteney, Spa and Empire hotels. Schools were requisitioned, and sites were also acquired at Foxhill, Ensleigh, and on Warminster Road, where offices were built that would double as emergency hospitals, should the need arise. The Empire was the last hotel to be given up by MoD (Navy), in the 1980s, but the MoD still uses its three out of town sites in Bath.

A site for the building of an ordnance factory had been selected at Puriton near Bridgwater in 1939 for the production of the explosive RDX. Construction work started in 1940, but because of technical problems and the shortage of suitable water supplies it was to be well into 1941 when construction work was completed. Production of RDX eventually started in August 1941, and the factory was soon producing much-needed explosives for the war effort. It is still in production.

The first bombs to fall on Somerset were a stick of four that were dropped at Flax Bourton, near Bristol, at 9.15 am on 18 June 1940, apparently after having been jettisoned. However, attacks on Taunton and Portishead soon followed, and on 25 June the first bombs fell on Bristol. From then until mid-December Somerset suffered bombing attacks on most nights. Daylight attacks were made to a lesser extent. On 15 July the first attacks on military targets in the county were made when RNAS Yeovilton was bombed; some buildings were damaged and there were five casualties. This was followed up later that day by a raid on the Westland factory at Yeovil, that hit the flight shed but caused little actual damage and no casualties. The first major air battle over Somerset occurred on 14 August, when a small force of Heinkel He111 bombers from 9/KG27 were intercepted while on their way to attack Cardiff docks. That afternoon, Blue Section Spitfires of 92 Squadron, then based at Pembrey in South Wales, caught the Germans at 15,000 feet over the Street and Glastonbury area. During the 15 minutes' running battle that followed, three of the Heinkels were shot down by the Spitfire pilots, of which Flight Lieutenant Bob Stanford Tuck claimed two, and damage to a third.

Bombing raids by the Luftwaffe during this period (later to be known as the Battle of Britain) affected Somerset almost as much as anywhere else. However, because of the rural nature of the county, damage to buildings and casualties was usually light. Also the German bombs often seemed to be dropped at random. Occasionally, Somerset towns were targeted, and on 14 August bombs fell on several towns and villages including Weston-super-Mare, Banwell, Burnham, Congresbury and Frome. Fortunately there were few casualties and little damage. The intense activity towards the end of August, however, was more damaging. Between 23 and 25 August, over one thousand high explosive bombs and incendiaries were dropped on Somerset towns. Five shops were demolished in Keynsham, many buildings were damaged in Cheddar and Wells, and incendiaries were scattered over Norton Radstock. Fortunately there were few injuries, but this was not true of the Bridgwater area, where ten people were killed and ten injured on the night of the 24th.

Raids continued over the following weeks, and ordnance was often jettisoned over Somerset by bombers which couldn't find their targets in South Wales. The climax of the Battle of Britain over Somerset occurred towards the end of September with a series of raids targeting the Bristol Aeroplane Company works at Filton. The first attack, on 25 September 1940 involved a formation of 58 Heinkel He111s escorted by Messerschmitt Bf110 fighters, which flew in over Somerset that morning from their bases in northern France. They passed over Yeovil at 1128 hours, heading for Weston-super-Mare, and then, at 1138 hours, just short of the town, turned east for Bristol. Fighters from 10 Group airfields were scrambled, but because of confusion caused by feints made earlier that morning to threaten Portsmouth, Portland and Plymouth, followed by an attack on Bournemouth, the main raid on Bristol got through unmolested. The Luftwaffe formation reached Filton at 1148 hours, and dropped over 100 bombs on the airfield and works. Substantial damage was caused to the factory, and 91 workers were killed, with a further 145 injured. Bombs also fell outside the factory demolishing and badly damaging 900 houses, killing a further 58 people, and injuring 154. Three of the bombers were shot down by local anti-aircraft defences, and four more were intercepted by British fighters on their return leg, along with four of the German fighters.

The Luftwaffe returned to finish off the Filton works two days later, their main force of 30 He111s preceded by 19 Bf110 path-finders and escorted by a further 27 Bf110s. Although the main force was intercepted by RAF fighters on their run-in over Dorset and Somerset and turned away, the Bf110 pathfinders did manage to get through to Filton and dropped bombs onto the airfield, damaging one hangar. They were then attacked by the Filton-based Hurricanes of 504 Squadron and, in a running battle, three of the Bf110s were shot down as they headed south. There were more German raids that day, which was the last during which significant numbers of German bombers were to cross the British coast in daylight. Of the 850 aircraft flown by the Luftwaffe, 57 were lost, most of them shot down by the RAF, which in turn lost 28 fighters.

A formation of ten Bf110 fighter bombers also set off to attack the Parnall factory at Yate, where Fraser-Nash gun-turrets were manufactured. They were escorted by a further 42 Bf110s and 40 Bf109Es. The formation crossed the coast and split to try to disguise their intended target, and the remaining 35 flew on over Radstock. The Hurricanes of 504 Squadron were scrambled and set upon the Bf110s as they were lining up to attack the Yate factory. The German bombers abandoned their attack, frantically jettisoning their bombs in an effort to evade the British fighters. As they withdrew to the south, they were attacked by the Spitfires of 152 Squadron from Warmwell and 609 Squadron from Middle Wallop, and then by the Hurricanes of 56 Squadron from Boscombe Down and 238 Squadron, also from Middle Wallop. Ten of the Bf110s were shot down, including that of the group's commander. One of the Spitfires was shot down and one Hurricane damaged during the encounter.

The first large night attack on Bristol was made on 24 November 1940. The shopping districts of Wine Street and Castle Street were destroyed, and three churches went up in flames. Two hundred people died that night, and 689 were injured. Bombs also fell in an arc to the south of the city, and across Somerset to Chard, along the line of the bombers' track. A second heavy raid on Bristol, on 2 December, resulted in 156 deaths and 270 injured, and another on the 6th caused a further 100 deaths and 188 injured. More raids followed in the New Year, Bristol being bombed again on 3 January, when, in a raid lasting 12 hours, 149 people were killed and 351 injured. On the following night, it was the turn of Weston-super-Mare, where 33 residents were killed and 69 injured. Considerable damage was done to residential buildings, and this was added to the following night when the German bombers returned. Hundreds more houses were destroyed or damaged, but this time there were few casualties.

On 16th January 1941 Bath was attacked, 79 high explosive bombs being dropped, along with over 10,000 incendiaries, and the following night there were widespread attacks over the county, including Shepton Mallet and Taunton. Although February was

Members of Bathampton Civil Defence Division c 1940. (Bath Blitz Memorial Project)

fairly quiet, March brought more attacks, and Bristol was hit again, 257 being killed and 391 injured on the night of the 16th. Bridgwater was attacked with parachute mines and Yeovil was bombed. Incidents occurred over Somerset almost nightly during April, and on the night of 11–12th, Bristol suffered two heavy raids, killing 180 people and injuring 382. Widespread attacks also occurred across Somerset to the south-west of the city. Frome was bombed, as was the centre of Yeovil, along with several other towns and villages, including Portishead, Peasedown St John, and Shepton Mallet.

This in fact turned out to be the last major raid on Bristol, and, despite a spate of raids during May, including four on Yeovil, by the time June came, the Germans seemed to have lost interest. The reason for this was that they were preparing to mount an offensive to the east and were pulling Luftwaffe units back in preparation for this. The Germans mounted Operation Barbarossa, a full-scale attack on the Soviet Union, on 22 June 1941. Although this event had the effect of reducing German attacks on Britain, they did not come to an end, the UK remaining one of the Luftwaffe's priority targets for the rest of the war.

It was, in fact, to return to Somerset the following year with a vengeance. The Baedeker raids were mounted on Hitler's orders specifically to target British historic towns and cities in retaliation for the bombing of medieval German towns by the Allies as part of their strategic bombing campaign. Baedeker was a pre-war tourist guide, and the historic British towns and cities listed in it such as Exeter, Canterbury, Norwich and York became targets for the Luftwaffe, as did Bath and Weston-super-Mare. Bath had been thus far relatively untouched by the bombing. As it had no strategic importance, it had no anti-aircraft defences and limited civil defence capabilities. German Pathfinders appeared over the city on the night of Saturday, 25 April, dropping flares that were quickly followed by hundreds of incendiary bombs. The attackers flew in low and fired their machine guns at Civil Defence workers, firemen, and ambulance crews. Once the fires were started, high explosive bombs soon began to follow. One of the first landed beside the Civil Defence control centre at Apsley House and put its telephone lines out of action.

The two local night-fighter squadrons, Nos. 87 at Charmy Down and 125 at Colerne, put up aircraft, but were unable to make contact with the raiders because of the limitations of their rudimentary radar sets. Hundreds of bombs rained down on Bath, and fires started all over the city. The raiders eventually departed, but, having returned to base, refuelled and rearmed, about 40 returned to the city a few hours later for another attack. On the night of 26–27th April, the Luftwaffe returned to Bath with a force of 65 or so bombers. Coming in again at roof-top height, the aircraft dropped more bombs to compound the damage that had been wreaked on the previous night. After 90 minutes they departed. Although the RAF night-fighters had flown, they once again failed to make contact. The only resistance was put up by the Royal Navy, which had positioned a Bofors gun at Foxhill Camp and fired a few rounds, albeit hitting nothing! The raiders did not escape unscathed, however. The RAF shot down five German bombers as they headed for home on the first night, and four on the second. At

Combe Down Rescue Squad 18th April 1942. (Blitz Memorial Project)

dawn on the 27th, Bath was shrouded in smoke from still burning fires. Rescue work went on for several days, although many of the city's inhabitants had left their homes during the night and slept out under countryside hedgerows to avoid further attack. The Bath Civil Defence squads were reinforced by teams from other Somerset towns, and by the Welsh Guards, the Royal Engineers, and the city's two Home Guard battalions. Some 400 men worked for the following week or more, undertaking rescue work – they rescued over a hundred people from the rubble – and restoring communications and public utilities, as well as dealing with unexploded bombs. Two members of the rescue teams, CSM T.A. Leslie of the Somerset Home Guard and R.N. Willey of the Civil Defence, later received the George Medal for their outstanding courage in tunnelling through wreckage to rescue victims, and five others received the British Empire Medal for their actions.

Bomb damage to Stanley Engineering Works, Bath 1942. (Bath Blitz Memorial Project)

The Luftwaffe dropped thousands of incendiaries and over 250 bombs on Bath during the Baedeker raids. The casualties have been put at 417 dead and 872 injured, 357 seriously. Over a thousand buildings were damaged beyond repair, and 16,883 others were damaged, but repairable. However, much of the centre of the city escaped serious damage. Although the Regency Assembly Rooms were destroyed and Bath Abbey lost much of its stained glass, the latter remained structurally intact, and the Roman baths along with many other of the city's architectural gems remained in one piece.

However, the Baedeker raids continued, and on the night of 28 June, it was Weston-super-Mare's turn. The first raid began at 0120 hours, not long after nightfall, as it was Double Summer Time. It was a moonlit night, and the first aircraft came in at low level to drop flares and incendiaries. They were followed by others which dropped high explosive bombs. Shops, churches, civic buildings and dwelling houses were destroyed or damaged. As the raiders left the Civil Defence squads took to the streets, along with the fire and ambulance crews. Personnel from the Initial Training Wing at nearby RAF Locking were also sent to help, and bomb disposal teams arrived to deal with a number of unexploded bombs found in the wreckage. The rescuers had not long finished working when, at 0150 hours the following morning, the air raid sirens wailed again. The Luftwaffe's raid followed the same pattern as the previous night, and the bombers flew over the town for 50 minutes. Weston's shopping centre was badly damaged, but the heaviest casualties occurred in the residential area around Orchard Street. Here there were many guest houses where newly-arrived visitors were staying. The wardens were therefore not sure how many people were actually in the wreckage. The rescue parties continued their work, reinforced by arrivals from other Somerset towns. Some 10,000 incendiary bombs and 97 high explosive bombs were dropped on Weston-super-Mare during those two nights, killing 102 people and injuring 338 (170 of them seriously). H. Cox received the George Medal, and one MBE and two BEMs were awarded to other rescue workers.

German raids continued after this, but were sporadic. They were, nonetheless, lethal. On the morning of 28 August 1942, for example, a lone raider crossed Somerset at high altitude and at 0900 hours dropped a single bomb on Bristol. It landed on Bread

Weir bus terminus and hit three buses, killing 48 people aboard and injuring 56. (This was the highest casualty rate for any single attack during the raids on Bristol.) The last civilian casualties to be caused by Luftwaffe action in Somerset were in the early hours of 15 May 1944, when a Junkers JU188 of 2/KG6 pursued by a Mosquito of 485 Squadron from Zeals jettisoned its bombs over Wincanton. One of these hit a building, killing one person and injuring four more. Shortly afterwards, at 0230 hours, the Junkers was shot down by the Mosquito, flown by Flying Officer John Hall and Flight Lieutenant Jock Cairns. Half an hour later, another 488 Squadron Mosquito, flown by Flying Officers Ray Jeffs and Ted Spedding, shot down the last enemy aircraft to fall in Somerset. This was a Dornier Do217 that came down at Camel Cross near Yeovilton.

There was no further enemy action over Somerset during May 1944, and very little between then and the war's end. During the wartime period a total of 668 people had been killed in the county as a result of enemy action, and a further 1,605 people were injured, 665 of them seriously. Some 35,000 buildings had been destroyed or damaged in Somerset during this time.

Not all of the German bombs were dropped with accuracy, but some were deliberately dropped inaccurately. An example of the latter were the bombs dropped by a Heinkel He111 pilot during the Baedecker raids on Bath. After having survived being shot down on the return trip, the pilot confessed to his captors that he had dropped his bombs short on the run-in to Bath, as he had been a student in the city before the war and still had many friends there.

Prisoners of War (PoWs) were also part of the wartime scene in Britain. There were eight POW camps in Somerset, at Colley Lane; Bridgwater, and Goathurst Camp nearby; Penleigh Camp, near Wookey Hole; Brockley, near Bristol; Barwick House, near Yeovil; Norton Fitzwarren (two), near Taunton; and Stoberry, near Wells. The majority of these were built during 1941, to accommodate the thousands of Italians that had been captured at Tobruk in North Africa. At first, the prisoners were kept under high security, but this was later relaxed and they were able to work on farms and subsequently were allowed to visit local towns – as long as they were back in camp before the pubs closed! A few German PoWs had appeared in Somerset and their number increased after the D-Day landings. They were segregated into 'white' (low escape

St. Bartholomew's church, Bath was completed in 1938 and virtually destroyed in the air raids of 1942. (Administrator of St Bartholomew's church, Bath)

risk) or 'black' (high escape risk) categories according to their political beliefs, and, although the high risk category prisoners remained under guard, the low risk prisoners were allowed off camp later in the war. Repatriation of PoWs started during the autumn of 1945, but some remained behind and settled down as British citizens.

With the entry of the USA into the war in December 1941, the first US Army units were moved to various parts of the country, but towards the end of 1942 Operation Bolero was instigated and this called for the majority of US Army units and some USAAF squadrons to be relocated in the South West. By then, there were few British Army units in the area, and so the Americans were able to take over vacant camps and depots. Bristol and Somerset were selected for a good number of these units. Taunton became the headquarters of the US V Corps, and the area around the town, including Norton Camp, became the base of the Third Tank Destroyer Group, along with a number of signals, ordnance, military police, and quartermaster units, as well as two elements of the Ninth Air Force. The US Third Armoured Division was one of four divisions to be based in the West Country. It established its headquarters at Redlynch House near Bruton, with its rear HQ at Wincanton, its 54th Armoured Field Artillery Division in Frome, and 143rd Armoured Signal Company at Cucklington. An anti-aircraft artillery brigade was stationed at Weston-super-Mare, and other units were located at such places as Milverton, Brean, Hallatrow, Blagdon, Martock, Bridgwater and Cheddar.

The Americans took over a stores depot to the east of the village of Norton Fitzwarren, and this was subsequently expanded into a vast site with dozens of large storage sheds with a network of railway lines to serve them. A huge fuel depot was also established by the US Army at Walrow, near Highbridge, along the Somerset and Dorset railway line.

Hospitals were also established by the Americans, not only to serve their camps, but in anticipation of high casualties that were expected following the invasion of Europe. In the Taunton area, the 810st Hospital Center was at Hestercombe House, the 67th General Hospital at Mosgrove Camp and the 101st General Hospital at Norton Camp. There were the 152nd and 160th Hospitals in Bath, the 121st and 169th in the Yeovil area, the 185th General Hospital at

Bishops Lydeard, the 74th at Tyntesfield near Bristol, and the 61st Field Hospital alongside the airfield at Merryfield. In addition a large blood bank was set up at Chilton Polden, near Bridgwater.

This 'friendly invasion' of Britain took place from the spring of 1942, and was to build up until the summer of 1944 as more and more Americans arrived in the country. They caused a culture shock to the local population. Although the Americans were generally well received, there were more than a few who resented their sudden appearance after the two years in which the British, suffering bombing and blockade, had stood alone against the Third Reich. Fortunately the US Supreme Commander, General Dwight D. Eisenhower, was pro-British. He encouraged his troops to get along with the locals and backed this up with suitable measures. For example, he made his commanders personally responsible for the appearance and behaviour of their GIs in the street. (The term GI originated in the First World War, when American troops in Britain had the letters GI (standing for 'Government Issue') prominently stamped on their webbing and equipment.)

As part of their campaign of friendly relations with members of the British population, the Americans made contact with local dignitaries and councils, as well as inviting people to dances at their camps. The US bases soon became 'Little Americas' as the GIs made themselves at home. They imported supplies in vast quantities, and many items found their way into the local communities, who saw varieties of food such as canned fruit that had not been available for years. The US Army set up the American Forces' Network, a radio station that broadcast the latest baseball and American football results, as well as the shows of entertainers such as Bob Hope and Jack Benny. The station also played jazz and swing that was popular not only with the GIs but also with the British public, who became regular listeners. The larger US camps had theatres where the troops could watch the latest movies or see shows put on by visiting stars such as Bing Crosby, James Cagney and Cab Calloway. The composer Irving Berlin also visited the US bases and starred in a show at Bristol's Victoria Rooms. Major Glenn Miller was another popular artist, who toured camps and air stations with his Army Air Force Band.

When the troops of the US Army departed during the summer of 1944 to take part in the invasion of Normandy and the follow up

Part of the Paragon, Bath, destroyed by German bombs in 1942. (Noel Harbutt, Courtesy of Museum of Bath at Work)

landings, they left behind many friends amongst the population of Somerset. As with so many British servicemen, many Americans were never able to return to Somerset to see in peacetime the county that they had known only in war.

The British public suffered much during the six long years of the Second World War, from the blackout and air raids to shortages and the rationing of food, clothing and fuel. The surrender of the German armed forces on 8 May 1945 marked the beginning of the end of war, and, when the Japanese surrendered in August, there was rapturous rejoicing in the streets. As men and women returned from service overseas they and the people that they had left behind them had to get their lives back together.

Most of the airfields of Somerset were closed within a year or so as their personnel returned to civilian life. Some of the airfields were to carry on for some years afterwards, and several are still in use today. The majority, however, were disposed of and are forgotten by most people. The occasional monument or memorial has nonetheless been erected, and accounts such as this appear from time to time, that will hopefully serve as a reminder to the older generations and also to inform the younger ones of the important role that the airfields and the people of Somerset played during the momentous events of the Second World War.

BIBLIOGRAPHY

During the preparation of this book I consulted many sources, including documents (both published and unpublished), books, and magazines. The following is a list of the main publications that I have used, and I am grateful to the authors for their earlier work.

Action Stations, nos 5 and 9, C. Ashworth, PSL, 1982

Adolf Hitler's Holiday Snaps, Nigel J. Clarke Publications, 1995

Aircraft of the RAF since 1918, O. Thetford, Putnam, 1995

Bomber Command 1939–45, R. Overy, Harper Collins, 1997

Bomber Squadrons of the RAF and their Aircraft, P. Moyes, McDonald, 1974

Britain's Military Airfields 1939–45, D.J. Smith, PSL, 1989

British Aircraft at War 1939–45, G. Swanborough, HPC, 1997

British-built Aircraft, Vol.2, R. Smith, Tempus, 2003

British Warplanes of World War II, editor Daniel J. March, Aerospace Publishing, 1998

Coastal, Support and Special Squadrons of the RAF and their Aircraft, J.D.R. Rawlings, Janes, 1982

Fields of Deception, C. Robinson, Methuen, 2000

Fighter Squadrons of the RAF and their Aircraft, J.D.R. Rawlings, McDonald Janes, 1975

Flying Units of the RAF, A. Lake, Airlife, 1999

Operation Bolero, K. Wakefield, Crecy, 1994

Pillboxes, H. Wills, Leo Cooper, 1985

RAF Squadrons, C.G. Jefford, Airlife, 1994

Royal Air Force – the Aircraft in Service since 1918, M. Turner and C. Bowyer, Hamlyn, 1981

Somerset v Hitler, Donald Brown, Countryside Books, 2001

Somerset at War, Mac Hawkins, Dovecote Press, 1988

Spitfire – the History, E.B. Morgan and E. Shacklady, Key Publishing, 1993

Thanks for the Memory, Mac Hawkins, Hawk Editions, 1996

The Source Book of the RAF, K. Delve, Airlife, 1994

The Squadrons of the Fleet Air Arm, R. Sturtivant, Air Britain, 1984

The Story of RAF Lulsgate Bottom, Ian James, Redcliffe Press, 1989

The Squadrons of the Royal Air Force and Commonwealth 1918–1988, J.J. Halley, Air Britain, 1988

UK Airfields of the Ninth, Roger A. Freeman, After the Battle, 1994

War Over the West, E. Walford, Amigo Books, 1989

Westland, David Mondey, Jane's, 1989

INDEX

SQUADRONS, UNITS ETC